THE TEACHINGS OF YAMA

THE TEACHINGS OF YAMA

A Conversation with Death

By

Janaka Stagnaro

NARROW DEER PRESS
SACRAMENTO 2014

Narrow Deer Press
3242 Marrissey Lane
Sacramento, CA 95834

Book design by Janaka Stagnaro

All art by Janaka Stagnaro

ISBN-1502728818

to All That Is

and to the living Silence

in me and all around me

CONTENTS

Think not disdainfully of death, but look on it with favor; for even death is one of the things that Nature wills.
—Marcus Aurelius

Come on, baby, don't fear the Reaper.
—Blue Oyster Cult

Only the man who no longer fears death has ceased to be a slave.
—Montaigne

As long as you do not know how to die and come to life again, you are but a poor guest on this dark earth.
—Goethe

To die, to sleep;
To sleep, perchance to dream—ay, there's the rub:
For in that sleep of death what dreams may come,
When we have shuffled off this mortal coil...
—Shakespeare, *Hamlet*

"Death is the only wise advisor that we have. Whenever you feel, as you always do, that everything is going wrong and you're about to be annihilated, turn to your death and ask if that is so. Your death will tell you that you're wrong; that nothing really matters outside its touch. Your death will tell you, 'I haven't touched you yet."
—Carlos Castanada, *Journey to Ixtlan*

If a man considers he is born he cannot avoid the fear of death. Let him find out if he has been born or if the Self has any birth. He will discover that the Self always exists...
—Ramana Maharshi

INTRODUCTION

In the spring of 2000 I had a dream. I have many dreams that I recall, and many of them I find insightful, inspiring and sometimes life-changing. This dream arose most vividly, a dream of death in the shape of a woman holding the rotting head of a child—her child—demanding attention. I awoke, not disturbed, but profoundly moved. Maintaining the Silence of my Being I immediately wrote a poem about it, which subsequently inspired the beginning of this book.

As with many poems I write, new insights arise as they take me to that Secret Place beyond the linear reasoning of the day-conscious mind. After writing the poem new images arose in my imagination. I took them into my meditation, and after abiding in the Silence of Being, the idea emerged that a book was to be born from the dream. It was to be titled, *The Teachings of Yama: A Conversation with Death*.

I felt thrilled at the idea. Yet no clear image about the book's content came forth. It was just a notion, similar to looking at a faint star. If I gazed at it directly, the book disappeared; yet if I sensed it out of the corner of my eye, with peripheral vision, the sense of the book would shyly reveal itself.

It revealed that I was just to write about what I love to talk about, what is only worth talking about: the Quest for Truth and how to go beyond the reach of Death; to bring forth the teachings of Ramana Maharshi, *A Course in Miracles*, and other non-dualistic teachings in a fun story form, that was clear and poetic; to write for myself, to have fun, and not to worry about what others may think. And to give up any concern about whether the ideas in the book were valid or not for those who might read it.

It has been the easiest writing I have ever done. Whenever time permitted, or when I made time, the words simply flowed. What I wrote would often parallel what was happening in my waking life, giving me guidance and insights, encouraging me along the way.

Like a dream this book is a collection of actual personal

experiences (whether in waking or dreaming consciousness), imagination, and stories and teachings of others that have become a part of how I express myself in the world. Many of the stories readers will recognize, despite my elaborations, with various ones coming from Hindu and Buddhist traditions. The teachings and teachers who have influenced me and thus this book have been, beyond the aforementioned Ramana and *A Course in Miracles*, to mention a few, are Joytish Harish and his teachings on the *Leela* game, *The Impersonal Life*, Karunamayi, Nisargadata, Rumi, *The Upanishads*, *The Bhagavad Gita*, Rudolf Steiner and his Waldorf education, the Buddha, and Life itself. As I have been synthesizing Eastern and Western teachings with my own experiences and realizations, along with this particular time and space I was born into as an American in the 21st century, so do the teachings of Yama reflect this.

This is not a channeled book by some entity named Yama. I was fully conscious through all of the writing. Yama is simply an Inspiration. A Focus. A Reminder. I cannot say that the Yama of this book is real or unreal, any more than I can say that this Janaka of this life is real or unreal. Does it matter anyhow?

Now some might question how death can be an inspiration, for Yama is the name of the Hindu god of death. Since childhood I have been fascinated with death. For a long while that fascination included all the usual metaphysical questions: Did life exist on the other side? Is there a heaven and a hell? How to contact the dead? Is there reincarnation? And on and on the questions came. Perhaps the first question concerning death happened when I was in kindergarten. My neighbor, Elizabeth, born on the same day and in the same hospital, died of leukemia. Why her and not me was a question I carried with me, and that question continued as I watched people die and others live. Why some died in an accident and not others?

It was not until I found myself in a near-drowning incident while canoeing down the Russian River with some college friends that death became a friend. My canoe capsized and in a panic, and not knowing how to swim at that point in my life, I attempted to swim upstream. Soon I was going down into the depths for the third and last time, my cries for help I believed unheard. I did not descend into the darkness of the river but into a quiet light. Then from above the scene my Awareness, like the Witness of a dream, watched my rescuer jump up from his spot on the shore and wade (afterwards I discovered that I was drowning in perhaps three feet of water!) into the river and grab my outstretched hand. Suddenly my Awareness was back in a coughing body that grudgingly thanked the man. I thanked him more out of politeness because I was not too pleased to be back encased in this heavy body.

Perhaps it was from this time on that I have lived with the notion that life is an adventure, and that when I die and review this life, I want it to be a good story. Who wants to watch a boring rerun full of grimaces and if-only's? With such a notion death is not something to meet at the end of one's life, but, instead, is a companion whispering, "Not much time left." Hence the two-fold nature of Yama: the Lord of Death and the Lord of Dharma, of doing one's duty or what Baggar Vance, the golf guru in the movie of the same name, spoke about of finding one's Authentic Swing.

When I did bodywork on men fading away with AIDS, many inspired me because they knew they were dying. Knowing they were dying they enjoyed everything to the fullest, that caress, that song, that morsel of pasta. We are all dying. We are terminally ill with the disease of living. Yet we pretend that we will live forever with these bodies, hiding away from the truth with our distractions and entertainments, looking away from the pile of bodies that are tucked neatly away in wooden boxes or quickly buried. Believing that life is actually being a body, instead of seeing the body as a vehicle of expression, we squeeze out every second with the use of medicines and machines.

Life has nothing to do with quantity of years, but with quality, of what you make of the time while having a body on this planet. As the Buddha said, one's life is wasted if one knows not who he is.

Yama reminded us all on September 11 that we need to wake up and live, to find the Essential. As the dust of the Twin Towers settled, people started looking around at the world and those in their lives with more appreciation, because tomorrow may not come, and the American dream of acquiring began to wobble and fade. But the powers of illusion are hard to dispel and soon those in high positions shouted that we must get back to normal. Act like a good American and get out there and consume. No one will make us change!

And as Yama points out, when distractions become so strong, his reminders as death are not always gentle.

This book is not for those who want to find out about what happens after one dies or drops the body. This book is for those who want to come to the Place where death never existed at all, who want to know the true Self, changeless and all encompassing. This book is simply a reminder that death and change are but friends when seen from the I of All That Is. Yama says in the book: "Your book will be a book of moments, of questions and answers. Many will find contradiction in my teachings. But contradictions are found in sequences, where the logic of the intellect reigns.

"To go beyond the place of death, of time, to the Truth, answers are for only the Moment."

May this book be an inspiration to you, dear friend. As with all teachings or with words from those "in the know," take from these teachings what feels right and leave behind the rest. If you find wisdom in these pages bless my teachers, especially my Ramana who quietly watches and waits. And if I have written untruth, may you catch it and give me pardon. All I can do is trust in the Great Process, and as a prayer in *A Course in Miracles* says:

I am here to be truly helpful
I am here to represent Him Who sent me
I need not worry about what to say
or what to do
For He who sent me will direct me.
I will be content where He sends me Knowing that I go there
not alone.
I will be healed as I allow Him to teach me to heal.

God is Great. And you are That which you seek. May you always remember and see God in your Self in the Self of All.

Janaka Stagnaro

WARNING: I have been told by some early readers prior to publishing that the first image of meeting Yama was very intense, so intense that there may be many readers who will turn away in horror and disgust. They suggested that I might consider changing the image to allow more readers to continue in order that more will have a chance to discover the spiritual gems awaiting.

So I considered it. But I have not changed the original vision of the dream. I believe it starts this way because this is how most of us view death—with horror. We do not want to look at it straight in its raw face. However, as in most mythic tales there waits a dragon or some other monster to face before the hero reaches the treasure or rescues the imprisoned. You, dear reader, whether you know it or not, are that hero or heroine; and you are on a journey as great as Persephone's.

The Teachings of Yama

Chapter I
Meeting Yama; helping the earth; temptation

I had a dream ... I dreamt I was on a stairway and below me stood a woman—a woman in rags holding in her arms the rotting head of a girl.

She cried: "My child, my child!"

In horror of the stench that filled my nostrils, I turned and fled upstairs.

She followed.

Through the doors of the finest restaurant I ran. "She comes! She comes!" I warned the hall full of diners. Yet no one heard my shout above the din of cutlery and rustling of conversation. Past the tables I fled, and as I began climbing the attic stairs, the woman entered, and the din stopped and silence reigned a moment before the screams of recognition prevailed, and panic became the dessert of the diners.

And only half-eaten dinners remained in the hall.

Into the attic I escaped, closing the door behind, hoping, praying, that the doorknob would not turn. Then the stench slipped under the door and the knob began to move. Into her sunken eyes I gazed. With nowhere to run I surrendered and sat down. I closed my eyes and closed my nose and silenced my breath.

I felt a tap on my shoulder. Come and drink with me, I heard somewhere in the distance of my mind. I opened my eyes and numbly followed her. We descended to the empty bar downstairs and she began making us drinks like some macabre bartender. And though the rotting stench of the head made me gag I accepted her drink, and took a respectful sip.

She smiled and said, "I am pleased with you, for you no longer attempted to flee and have accepted my drink."

"Nowhere could I run, so I did nothing but the inevitable. I no longer had the choice of fleeing," I replied.

"Ahh, the same is for the others; although they constantly create circumstances to provide the illusion of escape.

"Ask me a boon and it is yours," she said.

"Very well, tell me who you are."

She smiled.

"I am the plan of everyone and every remembrance.

"I am every exhalation.

"I am every burst of anger and every grievance held.

"I am the smile and promise of your career politicians, and the ambition of every man.

"I am the farewell of every lover and the meeting of another two.

"I am the screams of war and the riots for peace.

"I am the passing by of every beggar's hand and the opening of a savings account.

"I am the mouthful of every delicacy and every grumbling belly unanswered.

"I am the spewing of every vehicle and the soiling of every water.

"I am every footprint on the shore and every wave.

2

"I am in every kiss and in every copulation.

"I am in every museum and in every poet's dream of immortality.

"I am in every rifle barrel and on the edge of every knife.

"I am in every word of gossip and in every thought of judgment.

"I am every lie.

"I am in every candle flame and in every cloud and in every spring.

"I am in the bloom of every flower.

"I am in the shadows after every sunrise and in the center of every star.

"I am the pointing of God's finger. I am time.

"My name is Yama—I am death."

****

Yama! I caught my breath. It has come to this. I now face death, I said to myself. I felt both fear and awe.

She smiled and said, "Because you sought to know about another and were willing to listen, unlike the multitude too busy thinking of only themselves, I will give you another boon."

I saluted with folded hands to the one who is named Yama.

"Please, Revered One, you who draw nearer with every blink of one's eye, tell me of your child and why you weep."

"My child, throughout these thousands of darkened years, in the age called Kali, has been trampled by ignorant, hard-hearted men. They have enslaved her and have worked her lifeless. Their hearts empty of gratitude.

"By the fruits of their greed they have defecated upon her, and by their lust for power have drowned her in their own blood.

"And throughout this torment my daughter has given her all, never holding back.

"My child is the Earth itself."

Suddenly, the rotting head Yama held transformed into a miniature blue-jeweled sphere of the Earth. Then the Earth vanished, and with it the stench disappeared.

3

"Because you asked about my child who is dear to me and asked not to remove the stench for your own sake, ask of me another favor."

"Please, you who lead every youth onward, tell me how I may help your child," I asked, bowing once more.

"Very well, I will tell you."

She paused for a moment.

"Be aware. That's right. Be aware of all that you do, all that you see, feel, taste, smell and hear. See the shadows and how they stretch from stone to stone upon the path you walk. Hear the birds twitter amidst the hum of silence. Feel the warmth of the sun shining on your back and then the coolness of the passing of a cloud. Taste every morsel of food, savoring every spice, and taste the rain the same. Breathe in the smell of the barnyard with the same smile as you would sniffing jasmine."

I said, "Dear Yama, you who have been since the first movement of time, who knows the time-span of all things, I do not understand how this helps your child. Please elaborate."

"By being aware, you become awake. By being awake you will not trample ignorantly upon the Earth in your sleep. And by being awake you will become simple; for no longer will you have a myriad dreams to fulfill."

"Thank you, I understand more clearly. Yet, please explain that since you lead all things to destruction, why the need to help the Earth? It is doomed to perish."

Death replied, "Many a fool have thought thus, and have lived their lives for the moment, living to satisfy only their desires. Let me explain:

"The Earth is none other than your mother. Every need you have while expressing through a physical human body—a rare opportunity that countless souls desire to have—is given by her. And even as I quickly lead your earthly parents away, still every parent needs to be given gratitude.

"With every breath should rise gratitude. With every morsel of food, every whisper of the wind, every step, every touch of another creature, every sigh, every stab of pain, every beat of your heart, every laugh, every smile of a child, every bottle of wine to accompany a drunkard home.

4

"With all these and everything that comes, gratitude needs to meet them.

"This brings honor to my child and thus pleases me. And when I smile I do not work so hard."

****

Peering intently into the smiling face of Yama, I said, "Wait a minute. What you have just taught me sounds like you are asking all to be worshiping life. If you are death, how does worshiping life please you? I am confused. Are you truly death?"

Yama smiled. "I am pleased with your questions.

"I am indeed death. And I am life. I see no difference. In the darkest of winter, or in the middle of the greatest conflagration, life lies hidden. And in the blooming of spring and in every flowing river I wait. I am the death of every youth while life is the birth of every adult. We are two faces of the same coin."

In a flash the woman in rags was no more; and in her stead stood a majestic looking man, dressed as a king, with a mighty sword by his side.

"Ask of me anything," this kingly figure said in a very serious tone. "You can rule over the world—a benign king even, looking after all his people. I can make you the richest man in the world or the most intelligent. You can have any woman you want, or women, for that matter, and be adept at pleasing them all. I can make you famous, your name adored even in your own lifetime, and for all ages to come in whatever field you choose."

I shook my head.

"You can live as long as you like. Supernatural powers I give you. You may visit the Three Worlds. You may read every man's mind and be impervious to curses. With a thought you may create anything or destroy whatever you will. You may have a celestial maiden every night upon a bed of clouds with angels serenading you. You may fly or walk through walls or upon water. You may change shape at will, be giant or small, or be in any shape you want. You may have the power of invisibility."

Again I shook my head.

"I will make you a god. Even the king of gods!"

5

Falling down on to my knees I touched Yama's feet.

"Revered Sir with many forms, you who are king of time and who even lead the gods to destruction, I know you offered Nicheketas thousands of years ago such things. And he refused. He desired true knowledge. He desired to know your mystery and to escape your touch.

"Today you still exist and tomorrow in the ages to come you await humanity's arrival. Birth to death and back again — this wheel is tiresome and all beings are crushed by it. I, too, want to be taught by you your mystery and to know how one can escape your clutches. Please answer my questions truthfully and clearly is what I ask."

"Then drink up and we will go," he said as he helped me to my feet.

I drank it all and the drink's sweetness warmed my whole being.

"What is it that I have drunk?"

"You have drunken wisdom. For it is only the wise who face death."

Chapter II
Vision of the times; why does Man suffer? delusions

With a wave of Yama's arm we stood upon the top of a high mountain.

"Behold the world," Yama said. "A world with many worlds within."

I saw upon the plains below two cities; enormous, each spreading to the horizon. Dark smoke spewed into the air. The river running between them fouled with fish belly up, bobbing upon the surface. In each of the cities I saw youth donning black and wearing ornaments of skulls. They snorted white powder up their noses and shot hot fire into their veins, and copulated in alleys strewn with garbage; while their parents sat staring into glowing boxes flashing images of blood and rape into their minds. I saw distinguished looking men in shining conference rooms talk about destroying a forest to help increase their corporate take; while younger men in a warehouse talked about whom to rob and kill this night. I saw generals and colonels with their shining metals peer over maps and pointing their fingers at where to strike. I saw their armies line up between the two cities, and I heard the battle cries and the roar of their war machinery. Then I heard the screams of the wounded and dying, and the cheering of the victors. And I saw the blood, like a river, disappear into the Earth.

I turned away and looked at Yama. "Are these the ones who worship you? Are these your devotees?"

"No, these are not my devotees. They do not even honor me. They are the devotees of my shadow; for they worship only their puny selves, who move upon the Earth with greedy mouths, devouring all that they can. And so I devour them. They know not who I am, only what I appear to be."

"Then who are you, you whom all people fear?"

"Ah, who am I really? That is for the end of this dream.

****

"Now ask me another question."

"Why do people suffer?" Why all this pain?"

"Come with me and I will show you."

No longer upon the mountaintop, we stood behind some trees in a jungle entangled in vines. In front of us was a clearing into

8

which a well-beaten path led. In the middle of the clearing lay a pit.

"Why are we here?" I asked.

He held up his finger for silence. Suddenly the jungle reverberated from the trumpeting of elephants. Then I saw a man, his eyes wide in fear, running down the path looking over his shoulder to where the trumpeting sounds of the elephants issued.

"Oh, no!" I cried, ready to dash out. "The pit! The man doesn't see the pit!"

Yama held my shoulder. "Watch."

As I feared, the man fell unmindful into the vast pit. With one hand he caught hold of a thick root. The elephants came and ran around the pit in rage. For a moment he felt safe. Then he noticed at the bottom of the pit awaited an enormous serpent; its maw opened wide; its hot breath scorching the man's skin. Then he noticed on the root a rat, which ever chewed upon the root. Above his head he now heard the buzzing of a swarm of angry bees.

Just when the man was near despair and ready to let go, a drop of honey fell onto his lips. Tasting so delicious, so sweet, the man forgot his predicament, and holding tightly onto the root with one hand he held out the other to catch another drop of honey.

I turned away, for I could not bear to see the inevitable.

"Who is he? And what did it all mean?"

My guide looked at me and smiled, touching my chest. "He is you. He is everyone. He is anyone who believes he is but a body, a pitiful creature encased in decaying flesh.

"He runs upon the path of life, running through the tangled jungle of lifetimes of habits and impressions, likes and dislikes. The elephants are his desires, pursuing him, trumpeting in fear of non-fulfillment.

"The pit is hope.

"The root he hangs onto is his good deeds of other lifetimes. Gnawing upon it is the rat of time.

"Below him, in the vast, bottomless pit, awaits the serpent of passions, lust and anger. Buzzing around his head are the bees of his thoughts, ready to sting him any moment and send him down into the awaiting jaws.

9

"Yet the man forgets all these dangers, all this suffering, and holds on tighter, just for another sweet taste of pleasure the mind has made.

"Instead of running upon the path over and over again, falling into the same pit with each new lifetime, from that path he could leave. He could say that this path he wants no more.

"However, he remembers that taste of honey. And so he continues.

"No one causes man to run that path and to suffer."

****

I bowed to Yama in gratitude for this lesson. "How else are men deluded?"

He smiled. "Come with me."

We left the man to his fate and followed a path to a village. Upon the path lay a large rope. We saw a group of children running from the village in our direction.

"Quickly," said Yama, "hide behind these bushes."

As we crouched behind a bush he held onto one end of the rope. Unseen by the approaching children, he began to wiggle it. The children stopped and giggled. Then, one by one, with peals of laughter, they began to jump over the undulating rope, avoiding its touch.

Yama and I could hardly stifle our laughter at the joyous site of these happily playing children. Suddenly, we heard shouts of warning from the village. All the adults of the village ran frantically towards the children, gesticulating madly for them to come back to them. The children stopped playing and became silent. Mothers and fathers grabbed at their children's hands, and then roughly pulled the crying children back to the village.

We emerged from our hiding place. I looked at Yama with puzzlement.

Then I noticed an old man standing to the side of the path. He bowed to us with folded hands, smiling. He then turned, and with a shaking head, walked back to the village.

"Please explain to me, respected teacher, what I saw."

10

"What I held was the rope of creation, its fibers consisting of every world, every form made and to be made. Supreme happiness and outright joy made it dance and move. All movement is this joy.

"The children, seeing with the eyes of innocence, saw the rope for what it was, and quite naturally joined in the joyous dance."

"The adults," I asked, "what about them? They seemed afraid; except the old man."

"Indeed, fear was the lens through which they looked upon the rope. They saw not a rope, but an enormous serpent, ready to devour their children. The serpent of separation. Believing each to be separate from everything else, seeing themselves as their bodies, these adults can only look upon the world in fear. And the grabbing of their children and pulling them back to their village, to lock them in their classrooms to teach them about the serpent, they do in the name of love. Yet it is only out of fear. "And these children will grow up to be adults, wearing the glasses of fear."

"Yet that old man seemed different. He wasn't afraid," I said.

"The old man, eh?" Yama said, wearing a delightful smile. "There are a few—so very few—who do not look upon the world as a snake, but see it as it is, with the eyes of a child. These ones are no longer adults, nor are they children; although they will act as both at different times. They stand beyond anything we can say of them; anything we can call them.

"They are the ones for you to seek out, to keep company and to serve awhile. For they will see you as you truly are."

"Where are they?" I asked excitedly. "How can—?"

Yama raised his hands. "Wait, wait. All in good time.

****

Yama said, "You asked about delusions. "While there is only one delusion, it has many faces, and is not easily dispelled. "Look up the path."

I turned and saw a young man coming towards us with purposeful strides. He was dressed for a royal court of India.

Yama, who now wore, as I also found myself wearing, a simple white outfit of a renunciate, told me to go up to the man and to ask him where he traveled.

11

"I am the royal messenger. The king has sent me to find the prince, and to tell him that his father would make him now king," said the stranger.

At that moment a regal looking young man, although dressed in rags, came around the corner.

"That's him! That's the prince!" cried the messenger, running over to his object of pursuit, and then dropping to touch the prince's feet.

We stood by and listened to the messenger and saw the look of joy in the face of the prince.

"Tell the king, my father, that I come." And off ran the messenger.

Yama said to the prince: "So you are returning?"

"Oh, yes. It is time for me to come home."

Yama asked if we may accompany him upon the journey and the young man was grateful for the company. We walked a ways, the eyes of the prince focused on the path ahead. For a long while he walked thus, silent, seeing nothing but the path leading to his father. Suddenly, a twitch arose in his neck and involuntarily he looked over to the right. He saw, just off the path, a beautiful cluster of crystals. He fell to his knees to peer closer.

"How magnificent are these stones. I have never seen the like before. I must study them so that I may know these marvels of nature."

And so he sat, his focus completely on these crystals. For a long while we waited. Finally, Yama went over and whispered in his ears:

"Forget anything?"

"My father!" said the prince, slapping himself in the head. He jumped up, and once more with focused attention, walked upon the path toward his father.

Yet it was not long before another twitch arose and he saw to the left a group of celestial maidens bathing. And after some time of sporting with these heavenly damsels, again Yama had to go and remind the prince about his goal.

And so it was, again and again, twitches arising and the prince stopping to study animals, going into a library, learning a martial art, memorizing and chanting scriptures, going off on pilgrimages,

12

conversing with gods. On and on. We finally left him as he was learning how to cook.

"Will he ever make it?" I asked Yama.

"Oh, yes. Eventually. With my prodding. And if he learns to ignore those twitches."

"From where do these twitches arise?" I asked.

"Those twitches arise from habits of many lifetimes. They are like old interests bubbling up to the surface. Bubbles if you will. The challenge is to ignore them so as to let them pop. If you do not ignore them, it reinforces the habit and sometime down the road, again the twitch will arise. And even harder will it be to ignore."

"Will the king give up on his son and offer it to someone else?"

"Never. For the king forever sees the son upon the throne, and has all eternity to wait.

"The only one who suffers is the son, for my reminders are not always enjoyable, especially when he does not want to leave an interest. That is, if he becomes attached to his studies."

I bowed. "I understand. Delusion is all around. Vainly man goes here and there for something he thinks offers happiness; all the while finding suffering as its shadow.

"Yet are there not any who see through these veils?"

"Well, that brings us back to the old man and his kind."

Chapter III
Meeting the wise; discernment

We stood in front of a woman sitting with legs crossed, eyes closed, dressed in a white sari. She seemed not to breathe at all and a radiance of peace shone from her face. Yama stood over her and whispered into her ear; yet she made no signs that she heard. He returned to where I stood.

"What did you say to her?" I asked.

I told her she was missing out on life, so many pleasures going by. Then I reminded her of her family and all those who needed her and how she was abandoning them. Neither moved her.

Suddenly a group of men and women came up to her, each one carrying a savory dish, which they laid at her feet.

"Ah, my servants," Yama said. "Excellent cooks they are." The aromas from the food made my mouth water and stomach growl. However, she seemed completely oblivious to their presence. Then a young man appeared holding a bouquet of flowers. With great eloquence he sung poems to her in her honor, praising her saintly qualities. Still nothing happened.

When he disappeared a gang of urchins ran up to her and yelled a stream of abuse and even threw mud on her white sari. Their jeers and taunts elicited no response from her.

Yama waved his arm and the sun grew brighter and under it all began to welt. My breath seemed to dry my insides. However, the woman still sat unmoved. Another wave of his arm and the sky opened in a deluge of cold rain with still no effect upon her.

"How can this be?" I asked. "Is she dead?"

"We shall see." Yama's sword appeared in his hand, and holding the unsheathed blade, swung it at her neck. Through a flinching gaze I saw the blade past through her.

"She's a ghost!" I cried.

"No," he answered. "Quite the opposite. I cannot touch her. No thing can."

Onto his knees Yama, to my surprise, prostrated before the woman.

"She is a Liberated One, free from life and death, beyond all the pains of opposites. She is a sage, established in the infinite Self.

"Come and I will show you another Liberated One."

****

We walked into a royal courtyard. All around us people scurried about, being directed by a king. Gold shone everywhere, as well as gems of every color. Beautiful maidens surrounded him.

"Here is another one."

"This king?" I asked incredulously.

"Yes, this king."

"But he's totally different than the other one, the woman. Look at him, he's surrounded by opulence. Certainly he looks happy. Who wouldn't be?!"

"Let us see if he is really different," Yama said.

All of a sudden time began to speed up. Those maidens who were praising and taking care of him now began cutting him to pieces with their angry tongues, complaining about this, refusing to do that. Ministers whispered behind his back in conspiracies, their hands secretly dipping into the royal coffers. Upon a battlefield his once powerful army became routed, and the invaders stormed into the castle, flames danced about everywhere. The king sat upon his throne while all around people ran in panic. The invaders came in and made the king prisoner, throwing him into a dark dungeon. Years he spent in the darkness alone. Yet not once in all that time did the light in his eyes diminish. He looked at peace.

I said, "Despite all these calamities the king still looks happy. Besides his environment and the rags he wears he really appears no different."

"And so it is with the Sage, who is ever content, no matter where he appears to be. He may seem active or inactive, yet he is neither and both."

We both prostrated to the king.

15

Chapter IV
The making of a sage; discrimination

I asked, "Yama, you have shown me delusions and why men suffer, and have shown me ones who have conquered you; please, you the great teacher of all men, the reminder of how short our lives are, tell me how to become a sage."

"It is the most difficult state of being to achieve and yet the easiest.

"It is difficult, for all the world must be given up as worthless in providing happiness, all that one possesses must be seen the same. One must see that all things are transitory; merely ripples upon the pond of life.

"This includes the mind, the creator of pleasure and sorrow, of dreams and goals, of nightmares and monsters. To see the mind as not valuable in providing happiness and avoiding pain is most difficult of all.

"It is the easiest thing to do; for to be a sage all you need do is to be your Self, is to be your true nature."

"Well are not most of us being ourselves?" I asked.

"Yet, I look around at the world and I do not see any who shine with such peace as those two."

"No, most of those walking around are not themselves. They are slaves, told by their minds that this and that will bring them joy, and so they spend their waking moments thinking about what they have gained and what they hope to acquire.

"While the mind then whispers about those things to avoid, those people to fear, and dreams up so many schemes to avoid them.

"It is from the beginning that one seems to be born, the mind of the world—Maya—begins to spin its web.

"The adults, already caught in its power, direct all activity and thinking to teach the child that she is but a body. 'Oh, how cute you are,' they coo. 'Hurrah! You are two years old.' Etcetera and so on.

"And soon, around two to three years of age, the wisdom of her knowing dims in her eyes and she says: 'I want this; this is mine.'

"And for the rest of her life she will live in the delusion of the mind which has been programmed to believe that she is a body, and to take care of this body the mind tells her the things she cannot live without.

"Since she believes these things are expedient for her happiness, that she is not whole without them, for if she had them she would feel complete, deep down inside the mind lies with the belief that she is her desires.

"She must be if they would make her complete.

"And since the mind is her greatest need, for without the mind, she, that is her body, would be cut down by me, she believes that she is the qualities of her mind, as well.

"So all her desires, fears, habits, deeds, thoughts, feelings, appearances, talents, ambitions, knowledge, short comings, secrets, associations, friends and family, enemies, acquisitions, loss, and on and on, she identifies with.

"They become her in her mind.

"All that she says 'is mine' becomes her. She is lost.

"And then I come, her greatest fear, and tap her on her shoulder, and it is time to start all over again."

"And the Sage? What is the difference?" I asked.

"The Sage may not look differently on the outside; yet if you have the grace to spend time with her you will know the difference."

Yama pulled out his sword; the blade shining with a great light; its edge straight and sharp.

"This is the greatest sword of all swords, the mightiest weapon of all weapons. It can destroy the world and all worlds. It can slay demons. It can even destroy the mightiest of gods."

"What is its name?" I asked.

"Discrimination."

Yama said, "All those who look me in the eye and choose the path of the Sage, must learn to wield it. "The Sage wields it, slicing away all the mines and I am that's, uttering the sacred words: 'I am not this, I am not this.'

"All is cut away:

"All those people and things held dear, and all those repulsed and feared.

"Every event gone and to come.

18

"Every type of body in her life: the infant's, the child's, the youth's, the adolescent's, the adult's, the elder's and finally the corpse's.

"As well as every life past and every life to come.

"Every emotion that rises between joy and sorrow.

"Every thought, memory, idea, dream and fantasy; whether they be lofty or base.

"Finally she comes to the place of severing her Self from the notion I am."

"Well, what is left if she is not any of those things?" I asked.

"She simply is."

I nodded my head pensively at the sublime words of Yama. But my mind could not find anything to hold onto.

"Is what?" I again inquired.

"Is absolutely. Without any qualifications.

"Impervious to the touch of time, in the happiness and bliss of knowing and being the Absolute Truth.

"Becoming and being the One that has no other outside its Self.

"The one consciousness that resides in all beings and in all things; yet which cannot be pointed to because it is no object, no thing fixed in time.

"She is the Self of all selves."

"God?" I asked meekly.

"Yes. God.

"That state of Being has many names and no names, since no word can describe it. It is like describing colors to the blind or sound to the deaf; snow to a desert nomad or a kiss to a born hermit.

"All words are of the mind. And the place where resides the Sage is far beyond the mind."

19

Chapter V
*The secret language; the mind and breath and time; finding the
Silence in the madness; the danger of impatience*

Beyond the mind? What lies beyond the mind? I tried to ponder such a state, but could not. Not knowing what else to say to Yama or for that matter what else to think I just sat down and closed my eyes. I tried to go to that place beyond the mind, that place where Yama spoke of; yet my mind screamed at me, shouting at me to look at the possibilities of tomorrow for which to make plans, and in an instant it brought forward an old conversation I had recently with my boss and filled me with all manner of words I should have said, instead of the stupid ones I did, and then flew to a bedroom where lay naked a girl I had had a crush on and I saw myself ... then I heard my father's voice saying that no one knows the truth, so why listen to this one who calls himself Yama. Ignore his words. Live life. Don't fall for his lies....In a matter of seconds this barrage of the mind occurred. I opened my eyes.

"My mind! It's like a room crowded with people all trying to get my attention. How to subdue it, teacher? How to go beyond it? Tell me the easiest method."

"The easiest way? Find one who sits in the Self and stay in his presence as much as your deeds allow you to spend."

"Why should that help?"

"If you place together a group of violins and draw a note across one, all the violins, if properly tuned, will also reverberate with that note. So it is with being with a master.

"The Master or Sage sees you as you are; for the Sage is the Self of all selves.

"All your life friends and family and teachers, and everyone else, have helped form your definitions of your self, by seeing you in certain ways. Ways like being white, a male, such and such an age, poor, ugly or good looking, fat or thin, stupid or smart, etc.

"Yet all these definitions are cages.

"The Master holds the key of truth to free you.

"He may speak in words, and some of the words, like darts, may make it past the defenses of your mind and strike your heart.

"Yet most effective of all, if you are ready, is when the Master speaks in the most secret language of all, the language the mind fears most."

Yama stopped. I looked up and waited. And waited.

"Well?"

I finally said, "Is what?"
"Come and I will show you."

****

A man sat on a sort of divan, his head bare of hair. He wore only a loincloth. Around the man sat a group of people, some looking intently at him; others had their eyes closed. The man said nothing, his eyes staring straight ahead in space, a benign smile lightly playing on his face.

For a while we stood watching him and the others in their silence.

"What are they doing?" I whispered to Yama.

"He is instructing them about God and the Self. All their questions he is answering."

"Dear Yama, you are very wise I know, yet I hear nothing. There is only silence here,' I said.

"Exactly," replied Yama as he sat down and closed his eyes. "Do the same as the others. You might actually learn something."

With eyes closed I sat. The mind immediately sent forth a barrage of thoughts. However, something told me to just watch the thoughts, let each one go, and not to follow any of them.

Become aware of the space between the thoughts.

I watched my breath.

The more I watched my breath and became aware of the space between thoughts, my breathing slowed and with the slowing of breath my thoughts became fewer.

And soon breath, thoughts, and time seemed to cease all together.

After perhaps a long while of bathing in this living silence, I felt a tap on my shoulder. I opened my eyes and saw Yama smiling down at me.

"What peace," I heard myself mutter.

****

Suddenly, as though I was standing next to a cannon, I heard a blast, followed by another and another. These thunderous blasts

22

that shook me to my very core were the horns of cars. I found myself standing on a street corner in the middle of a city, skyscrapers all around. Yama stood next to me smiling and wearing a business suit as was I.

"Where are we? What happened to him and the silence?" I asked in despair.

"He and the silence have gone nowhere. Nor can they. Only you have appeared to have gone anywhere."

"Will I see him again?"

"Ahh, the eyes. How people rely on them so. Perhaps. If you mean seeing his body with which you are identifying him. Time and space does not confine the Sage.

"Anyway, tell me what you learned from him?"

We sat down on a bench. "Well, while no questions were spoken at all, all my questions disappeared. Only silence remained."

That now familiar smile grew on Yama's face.

"Silence!" I said excitedly.

"Silence is the answer. Silence is the language of the Master."

"Good. What else did you learn?"

"I learned that by just watching my thoughts and not being led by them they slowed down. The same with watching my breath. That there is a connection between breath and thought somehow."

"And ...?"

"Time!"

Yama nodded his head.

"Breath is the mind's food. When thoughts are few little breath is needed.

"And in terms of time, all come onto the earth with an allotted number of breaths, the number of which I know to the very last.

"Those who are anxious about the world with their minds racing or those who are panting in the throes of lust or those whose chest heaves with the flames of anger, all of them quickly use up their allotted time.

"Now there are those who can stop their breath by utilizing ancient practices and live in their bodies for hundreds or even thousands of years, until they breathe again."

My eyes grew wide in amazement.

"A thousand years is nothing to death. I always will be waiting. Such a trick is not the goal, for they wake up with the same desires, the same little self that went into the trance."

"Is it not good to have your breath stop then?" I said, confused.

"If it happens naturally it is best. Nothing needs to be forced."

****

I thanked Yama for his teachings on breath.

"If one does not have the grace to sit at the feet of a master, what are other methods to help one to come to that place of silence — to come to the place beyond your reach?"

I looked around me at all the rushing to and fro of pedestrians, and upon the drivers gripping their steering wheels of their cars.

"And is it possible at all to find that silence amidst all this confusion?"

"Your questions are worthy." Gesticulating towards our surroundings Yama continued, "It is possible to find peace amidst this clamoring; although it is far from easy.

"However, to truly find that eternal silence it must be unconditional, and thus it must be found everywhere. Even here.

"If there is but one inch of earth where you cannot find peace, one speck in all the worlds, whether in the highest heavens or in the lowest of hells you will become shaken in your core.

"And I will grab you.

"If you have been graced to meet a master and she has instructed you in meditation, follow the instructions unfailingly everyday. Start the day with it, greeting the sunrise established in silence. And again do so in the evening.

"If one has not that grace it is effective and safe to do as you did, watching your breath and thoughts, becoming aware of the silence around them."

I interrupted, "What do you mean safe? Can meditation be dangerous?"

"Nothing is dangerous to who you really are.

"However, there are dangers of delay to realization along the path for the seeker. There are more forceful breathing techniques and concentration exercises that—without a worthy teacher who is guiding each step of the way—can unleash forces from the subconscious that can wreak havoc in one's life.

"Delusions as well as great fears can overwhelm and overshadow one's life.

"A 30-watt bulb cannot take 100 watts without damage. So, too, someone who is not prepared on all levels cannot take the power of the Cosmic Self without some short-circuiting.

"Look around you. See all these people rushing to the next sale, to pass the car ahead, to grab a quick meal. These are those who will fall into my traps when they begin to consciously tread the path to escape their suffering.

"They have no patience.

"All their desires demand to be gratified instantly. They will go to those who shout that their method is fastest. They will pay lots of money for the quick way.

"At worse, they will do some 'fast' technique or do some mind-altering drug and blast their nervous system and become a useless member of society. At best, they might get a divine vision or two for their spiritual resumes.

"Most likely, however, they will go from teacher to teacher, method to method, continuing only to remain in my grasp.

"Like miners are these seekers, digging here and digging there, never having the patience to go deep enough to hit the Mother Lode.

"Some will stop in each shallow pit to pick up the shiniest stone and then pronounce to the world that they have found the truth.

"While others will find only dirt and gray stones in these shallow pits and will, after a while, filled with despair and doubt, will drop their spades and will lie down in what is now a grave. And then live the rest of their lives scoffing at the other diggers."

"Revered teacher," I said, "you have spoken of meditation as a way beyond you, please name another way."

Yama beckoned for me to follow.

25

Chapter VI
Devotion; the power of God's Names

As was becoming a normal occurrence in this dream, the scene suddenly changed. This time we stood in another palace, yet in a palace beyond any type I had ever heard of. It was filled with a soft radiance. Upon a golden throne sat a divine being, who appeared to be the source of the light. Around him attended splendid beings of celestial demeanor.

"Lord Vishnu," whispered Yama to me, as he bowed before the great one.

"Lord Vishnu?" I replied, prostrating, amazed that I would have the grace to actually be in the presence of the Great Preserver. Then to the throne walked a man with a brilliant halo around him. He carried a vina, an ancient stringed instrument of India, and prostrated to the Lord.

"Narada, my beloved," said Lord Vishnu, "you who dwell eternally in my heart, the immortal sage and musician. You please me how you go from world to world and time to time, singing of my love. Ask of me a boon."

"My Lord, you who are my all, I want only to know that I am your greatest devotee, that there is none who worships you more. That is all that I ask."

The Lord was silent for a moment.

"Alas, my dear one, there is one who is even greater in his devotion," the Lord said smiling.

Narada's jaw dropped in shock and stuttered that he would like to meet this great devotee. The Lord consented and invited us to accompany them.

Invisibly we stood in a modern apartment. At a table sat a man with his four children and wife. As he broke the bread he gave thanks to Shiva, a tear trickling down his cheek. Then we sat inconspicuously in the back of the bus he drove. All morning we followed him and watched him praise again Shiva for his lunch. Again he shed a tear. We continued following him the rest of the day until it was time to be with his family for dinner. Again the praise and the tear, and off to bed he retired.

"Ahh, my greatest devotee. I am so pleased with him," said Vishnu proudly.

Narada turned to me and asked, "How many times did he speak Lord Vishnu's holy name?"

A little startled I said, "Well…umm…none."

"Precisely," said Narada, a little smugly perhaps.

"All divine names are my name," said Lord Vishnu, "just as every being is called many names at different times; as a man may be called son, my child, student, husband, my dear, etc."

"Very well, I understand what you say, my Lord," said Narada, "that's all very fine."

He turned to me again. "Well, how many times did he say Shiva?"

"Three, I believe."

"Precisely!"

Lord Vishnu smiled in that way Yama would often smile at me when he was giving a lesson.

"Perhaps I was mistaken. Anyway, I have this urn of holy water I need for you to carry and place in a cathedral in the next town. It's not too far away."

A large urn appeared, nearly filled to the brim.

"I will gladly take it, my Lord, even if I have to carry all the way to Brahmaloka," said Narada, who was always ready to please his Beloved.

"Thank you," continued Vishnu.

"By the way, just make sure not one drop spills. This water is very dear to me so that all my worshipers may get my full blessing."

Vishnu disappeared. Thus Narada placed the urn on top of his head, and with slow deliberate steps, made his way across town. All day and into the evening it took, until finally he set it down inside the cathedral.

We had followed him all the way, and while there were some close calls, not one drop did spill.

Narada turned to us and said, "See, it is done. And not one drop spilled, fulfilling my Lord's request."

"Well done, my beloved devotee," said Vishnu who had just appeared in front of us. "Not one drop spilled I see."

Narada beamed.

And though Narada beamed, I had this funny feeling inside that he was being set up.

"Tell me, my beloved one, how many times in your day's labor did you speak my name?"

Narada blushed. His lips moved soundlessly. And then he fell down to his knees, like a tree felled by a mighty stroke.

"None, my Lord, I am ashamed to say."

"Precisely!" smiled the Lord. And the two divine personages disappeared, leaving us behind.

****

Yama looked at me and asked:

"Do you understand?"

"I believe so. The Lord showed that doing one's duties in the world and thinking of the Lord is extremely difficult."

"And...?"

"It seems more pleasing to God to be working in the world and thinking of him than spending one's time removed from the world."

"Perhaps," said Yama.

"However, does thinking of God only three times in a day that efficient?" I asked.

"Well, the Lord was making a strong point to his devotee. For one thing, the man worked without thought for himself, serving his family unselfishly.

"Yet there is no difference between sound and form; for out of sound forms arise. All this world is but vibrations— particles of light dancing to the great Om, the Primeval Sound.

"Name is also sound. And the Names of God is the same as form. Thus when one speaks the Holy Names, one actually forms the Lord on one's tongue.

"So even three times invokes God to form one's life. Now to work in the world and to think of the Lord all the while, with every breath, one is sure to escape my wheel."

Chapter VII
Developing character; practicing the virtues; Absolute truth versus relative judgments; harmlessness

I bowed and thanked my guide.

"You have illustrated well the efficiency of thinking of God and uttering his holy names. Please tell me how else one can escape the attachment to life and death."

"I am pleased with your earnestness. I will continue, for any teacher wants to enlighten a worthy student.

"As a river needs to have strong high banks to channel the waters of the thaw of spring, so as not to lose its power to reach the sea (the goal of all rivers) in the dispersal of a flood; so too must an aspirant develop character."

"Please explain what defines character."

"To develop character, one must cultivate the following virtues:

"Patience.

"Without it a man is restless, always on the move, agitated and anxious, the mind is as a bird tossed upon the winds of a storm. The moment is never realized, living only in tomorrow's hopes.

"With patience a man is calm and will become fertile soil for the seeds of Grace to be planted.

"From patience will grow faith, as a farmer knows that by watering and caring for his crop a harvest will soon be had.

"For faith is the knowing that in the calmness of patience only good can be gained, which follows a law set by God.

"And with that faith comes trust.

"Without trust a man burns in fear, and all around him I place mirrors to reflect his frightful dreams, and all the world seems to carry swords to make true his mistrust.

"Yet with trust, I will remove all mirrors, and the sweet pastures of the world will begin to be seen; for he will begin to see his glorious divine Self, that is both within and without.

"Arising from trust is contentment.

"Contentment is not complacency as many will be misguided in believing. Complacency gives birth to sloth and sloppiness; whilst contentment leads into gratitude.

"All that comes to the aspirant is seen as coming from God. All of the world is blessed by such a one because everything is seen as divine.

"From gratitude flows cheerfulness.

"Everything, being of God, arouses joy. And that joy takes flight and flies like a butterfly from person to person, pollinating cheer in everyone.

"The world is so full of shadows. Cheerfulness dispels all of them.

"These virtues must be cultivated. Cultivate one and the others will follow; for as in all things the whole is found in the part if you go deep enough."

"I thank you for your speaking of these virtues. Are there more to help one end one's suffering?"

"Indeed. Listen well.

"Practice kindness to all beings.

"Not only in deeds, but in words and thought. Harm none. See everyone as your closest brother.

"When speaking, always spread the truth, yet speak it kindly, and only when asked for, or if a situation requires it.

"And if a thought of ill arises, of judgment, counter it immediately with a blessing.

"Thoughts create the world. If all the people in the world thought kindly for just one day I would no longer have this job of death."

"Dear sir," I said, "forgive my question; yet those who have seen their family killed, or for that matter all those who have seen their loved ones taken away by you, no doubt would say that while you espouse kindness, you are no way kind in your actions."

"What you say is maybe true. However, in truth, I'm simply a servant of man. What man thinks, says or does, each one being a seed, I take and plant in time, and I become the fruit for every man to eat.

"Only man is free to be kind or not.

"The gods and demons only do as directed by the Universal Will or Mind. Man, in the relative scheme of things, stands in the middle between god and demon.

"This is why he makes such a mess of things and I have to do all the cleaning up—a thankless task, let me tell you!"

"Thank you. So really you give to each what they believe they want and what they believe to be true."

"Yes," said Yama, looking pleased.

"Please tell me more virtues to cultivate."

"Practice truth. Always.

"All the worlds rest on Truth. There is no difference between truth and God. There exists in the apparent chaos of the universe an order.

"If for a moment God was false, gods would become demons, demons into gods, the sages would speak lies and the satiation of desires would be the ideal for all to aspire towards.

"Inside would turn outside, thick would become thin, and all would be paradoxes."

"But wait a minute," I said, "it seems that the more one nears the truth, paradoxes are everywhere, such as to be rich is to be poor, to be first is to be last, etc., etc., etc."

"You're right. However if God was to be false all true paradoxes would not be paradoxical anymore. So the rich would be rich and to be first would actually be first."

Yama smiled. "Understand?"

"No—but that's okay," I said quickly, my head spinning with paradoxes of paradoxes. Such as if God was false then when inside would become outside—which is a true metaphysical paradox—what would that mean? Would the normal outside, which in truth is the normal inside, turn into the false outside? And if that was true then...I forced my mind to stop chasing such notions.

"Right. I trust that truth is all important! Please continue."

"A difference between a man of truth and someone of the world is that the former does everything he says, says everything he thinks and thinks only what is true. Rare is such a one."

Yama continued, "To know the truth is to sharpen the sword of discrimination between what is valuable and what is not."

"To distinguish the valuable from the invaluable is not always easily discernible," I said. "For instance, I may be starving and give away my gold for a loaf of bread; and then again I may give up eating a meal so I may buy a book I deem needed for my growth."

"Your examples only show that in the world one thing may be valuable for one moment and then worthless the next. There is nothing in the world that is not that way.

"An army may be valuable one moment for a country and the next be a financial drain; a husband may be valuable to have for some woman as a source of security, only to become a restriction for her freedom; to win enormous wealth may be valuable to fulfill one's desires and to live comfortably in the world, yet if the poor revolt the same wealth may be one's death.

"What I mean by valuable is only that which holds its value throughout time, untouched by the inflation of time and the fleeting desires of the mind."

"Well," I said, "that only leaves God, for there is not much outside of time. Only the eternal would be outside of time."

"There you go. Now that is wielding the sword of discrimination.

"Only the permanent is valuable. The eternal truth is that only God is valuable.

"All that is fleeting is false. The transitory offers nothing valuable, nothing of substance.

"Taking joy by obtaining some thing is like a man believing the sweet words of a prostitute.

"The wise constantly meditate on what is valuable and what is not, and cut away from their attention the false."

"Then does one ignore the things of the world? Do the wise avoid everything that is transitory?" I asked.

"Of course not, that would be silly and highly impractical, not to mention impossible.

"The wise are only concerned with the Eternal Substance, God, the Self, the Noumenon, the Absolute Being. In that way they are not fooled by the promise of things to fulfill them, to make them happy.

"By being focused on only Absolute Happiness they can truly enjoy all that is transitory because they can let them come and go without restrictions and grief."

"Thank you. Please tell me more," I implored.

"Harm none in thought, words or deeds. For when one knows the truth that only God exists and thus all is God and in God, thus the idea of separation has no basis of reality, why would one harm another? Why would one cut off one's hand if it drops the ball?

"Every creature is part of the body of All That Is."

****

"Dear Yama, I understand that it is wise not to harm anyone or anything being that we are in truth One Self."

"Good. Very good."

"However," I continued, "how can one avoid harming? Just breathing I destroy unseen creatures. Do you suggest we all become as some Jains who sweep the ground before each step lest

33

they step on an insect and who cover their mouths not to suck any in?"

Yama smiled. "There is a difference between harming and hurting. To harm is to intentionally inflict pain or death onto another with malicious intent.

"Hurting is simply being an instrument in the hands of time. Everyone who is attached to the form of the way things should be will suffer, will experience hurt.

"Look at that couple." Yama pointed to a man and woman sitting on a park bench, holding and caressing each other with their whole beings glowing with passion. "In a few months time he will need to choose between going away to college as was planned by his parents or staying with her. Either way she or his parents will be hurt; yet he is harming neither for his intent is not to inflict pain.

"He will be only making a choice in time."

"What about eating?" I asked. "Something must die in order for me to eat."

"In truth nothing dies.

"Death is only bodies changing forms, as the wise know. All is God. All is the One Self—the All in All.

"How can God kill God?

"How can God be killed?

"However, before one is firmly established in that Awareness, when one still flinches at a swinging sword or runs from a raging bull, eat as subtly as one can.

"Animals are densest and closest to humans. They feel pain, suffer fear, and some of the higher forms possess self-awareness. Eating such creatures harms them and harms oneself, for the feelings of the animals, their propensity to flee or fight, adds fuel to the feelings of me."

"Dear Yama," I asked, "do not many traditional cultures eat meat? And is it wrong for them to do so?"

"Yes, many cultures have eaten meat and killed the creatures in a sacred manner that created a conscious partnership between man and animal. And in some areas of this earth, man can only exist by the flesh of animals.

"Yet in this dark age beasts are cut down by machines after living a life of trapped horror.

34

"There is nothing sacred in this, no sharing, no gratitude. Only murderous greed. It is intentional harm. Eating these poor creatures one eats fear and greed.

"So while there is still a sense of feelings with vegetation, as they have a reaction to pain, there is no sense of me at all.

"Plants are like the hair of the earth. Still gratitude needs be given in the growing, harvesting and eating to please me.

"As plants are more calm than the ever-watchful beasts, and as you are what you eat, eating vegetation assists in having a calmer mind."

"So it is good to be a vegetarian," I said, feeling good about myself that I had chosen the right path years ago.

Yama shook his head and wagged a finger at me. "Become nothing. Be nothing. Being a vegetarian is but a cage. It can be a means. It is no end. And with every individual there are special needs. It is better to eat meat with humility and gratitude than to eat a piece of broccoli with pride or fear that if you do not eat vegetation you will fall spiritually.

"It is simply that eating plants instead of animals will help most assist the mind in becoming calmer and helps create less harm on this planet."

Chapter VIII
Between extremes; wanting the truth

I again thanked my teacher and asked for more virtues to be cultivated. We stood now in a long hall with doors to the left and right.

"Where are we? What's behind the doors?" I asked.

"Pick one."

I chose the first door on the right. Inside was a monk. He held in his hand a knotted rope in which he struck himself, his eyes sunken from lack of food and sleep.

"Please, sir," I said to him, "why do you whip yourself?"

"I am a great sinner and the temptation of the flesh is terrible. Only by subduing the senses and denying pleasure to the body can one reach heaven. "Fast, sleep not, look upon no woman, and storm the gates of heaven!"

Silently I closed the door leaving him thumping his head upon the floor.

"Try another door," Yama said, "on the left side this time."

I did. I saw a woman wearing a silken dress, richly adorned with jewelry in a plush room. She lounged on pillows, fed and fanned by male servants.

"Come in," she said to me in a languorous voice. "Eat." She pointed to the vast array of savory dishes in front of her. She leaned forward, obviously not shy about her revelations.

"Eat and then...."

I closed the door. Yama smiled that teacher's smile. Down the right side I opened a multitude of doors. One had a naked man standing on one leg with a long needle through his cheek; another had a woman walking around a statue of some god, only stopping to sleep a moment or two or stopping to eat a mouthful of food; another had a group of men with scriptures in their laps, all silently reading throughout the day; another had a yogini, with the sun overhead, sitting in a ring of fires. Countless doors on the right stretched down the endless hall.

On the left side, behind one door was a couple in sexual embrace doing complicated rituals and positions throughout the day; another had a group of people eating magic mushrooms and staring into space and laughing at their visions; behind another door was a man of great physical stature, lifting weights in a gym; while behind another door a woman twisted herself into all kinds of bodily knots.

And on and on the doors on the left continued.

After a while I stopped opening doors. "What did you see?" my guide asked.

"I beheld people engaged quite seriously, quite intently in some activity or another. Some, the ones on the right perhaps, seemed to be engaged in activities that were more traditionally spiritual, less oriented on the body."

"Indeed," Yama said, "all those you beheld were extremely engaged in an activity. However, neither side brings one closer to the Awareness that is beyond my reach, for they all are focused on their particular activity.

"Remember, all activity is in the realm of life and death. If one becomes too one-pointed in an activity there is great danger of attachment to the activity and identifying oneself as the action.

"For example, those practicing asceticism may call themselves 'ascetics.' That becomes their definition.

"When the ever-flowing life wants them to be evolving into other activities they will not be able to because such activities go against their definition of being an ascetic."

"Which is what you were saying about being a vegetarian," I interjected. "Being a vegetarian is one of those traps, yes?"

"Yes. And instead of just Being in the life flow they become rigid and I have to cut them down.

"That is why moderation is best. Then one can walk down the hallway and not get stuck in any room."

"Moderation in all things?" I inquired.

"Yes, in outward activity. Ye not in terms of inner movement.

"It takes constant vigilance of the mind and directing it to the Awareness to reside in That which you always are.

"The inward fervor needs be greater than any of those persons in the hall with their pursuits."

"I think I understand. Although can you demonstrate how intense one must be inwardly?"

37

With a wide grin on his face Yama walked behind me. Suddenly I felt one of his hands close my nose and the other close my mouth. Frantically I struggled to remove his hands and to gain a breath. I struck out with my fists; I tried to bite, thinking only of getting a breath. I wanted only to breathe once more. I wanted only that. And to gain that one breath I would offer anything in the world. Nothing in all of the world could be more valuable.

Then the hands were gone from my face and air rushed in to fill the void in my lungs. I gasped. When I had had my fill of air I accusingly asked Yama if he wanted to kill me.

"Well after all I am death." He smiled. "No, I was just answering your question.

"You must want God or the Self as much as that air. You must have the realization that only That gives you life.

"All else, all activities, are nothing compared to That.

"Without That you can do nothing."

Down on my knees I fell, tears flowing in streams.

"Oh Yama, I touch your holy feet for that lesson. How easy is it to forget that God is even more precious than air. And as air is all pervasive it is easily forgotten, easily taken for granted, as so is All That Is. Oh blessed are the moments when one breathes in God with remembrance and gratitude."

"Yes," said Yama, "and in such times one can even feel God breathing in you."

Chapter IX
Right action; the maze of the mind

"Dear Teacher, you brought me into that hall where individuals were engaged in activities and showed me that they do not lead one from your grasp. Is there any activity that aids in developing character?"

"Of course, but engaging in activity, no matter what the action, one needs to give up the idea that I am doing it. "Selfless service is best, which entails not dwelling on what is to be gained, as well as doing one's best."

"Does this work need be philanthropic, like feeding the poor?"

"Certainly feeding the poor and such other kind, caring work is good to do. It will help open one's heart and allow it to expand beyond the limited needs of one's self into the greater needs of others.

"However, let me show you something."

****

We stood in a balcony of a palace looking down upon a great garden. In the middle of the garden was a maze of hedgerows. Very complicated was the design, with twists and turns and lots of dead ends. In the center was a circle. And in that circle, written in the bloom of flowers, was the word 'Buddhahood.'

Standing on high I could see various individuals wandering lost in the maze in their search for the center. I shook my head in dismay at their plight, for the maze seemed impossible.

"Is it possible to reach the center?" I asked.

"Keep watching."

Then I noticed a man in simple work clothes carrying a few garden tools. He walked with calm steady steps upon a narrow, well-worn path (totally unseen by the other frantic seekers) that led from the periphery straight to the center. Occasionally he would stoop to go through a small opening in one of the hedges.

"What is that path?" I asked.

"Oh, that? It is simply the path the gardener takes every day to do his work in tending the flowers."

"You mean gardening is the direct path to Buddhahood?" I asked incredulously.

"No wonder I work so hard as death," said Yama, shaking his head, "the way you humans take things so literally! The next thing you know you will be starting a new religion where everyone must become gardeners and wear golden hoes around their necks.

"The gardener does his duty tending to the flowers daily. Unlike the others in the maze he thinks not about reaching some enlightened state in some far off moment, nor does he think about where he has been.

"He is simple. He does what needs to be done. Without complaint. Without thinking. He tends to the flowers and does not think about home. He goes home after his duties and does not dwell on the flowers.

"The maze is nothing but the mind that constantly creates an amazing world to fascinate and hypnotize, creating dead ends and winding pathways.

"Look closer at the maze."

I did. From a trick I learned as a child I tried to follow a pathway from the center to the beginning at the periphery. Immediately I saw the reality that those seekers found themselves in.

"Hey wait a minute! There is no way to reach the center by the maze. Each path from the periphery only leads to dead ends or to other paths that lead to the same. It's hopeless!"

"Such is the mind."

Chapter X
The three qualities of the mind

"Dear Yama," I said after pondering the last lesson, "you have shown that the mind cannot be relied upon to lead one to the truth, and you have stated clearly that no activity can bring one to That which is beyond.

"On the other hand, you teach that virtues need to be cultivated to prepare one for Self Realization.

"This seems paradoxical. Please clarify."

"While the mind cannot lead one to That, to God, it can reflect That, if free from desires, safe from the storms of passions.

"Come."

Yama transformed us into two crows perched upon a branch of a tall tree in a forest. Below us on a path walked a man. Suddenly three robbers jumped out from behind the trees; one dressed in black, one in red and the other in white. The one in black grabbed the scared traveler, brandishing a wicked sword.

"You have come into our realm. For that you must die."

And so the robber led the man into a dilapidated hut. We flew to the windowsill. Inside was dark and we could barely make out the man stretched on the floor with all his limbs tied. Upon the traveler's chest the robber in black placed a large weight. Laughing at the poor man's plight, he left the hut. Day after day he came, adding more weight each time, until it looked as though one more time would crush the breath forever out of the man.

Then one day, while the one in black was absent, the robber in red, carrying a whip, came in and removed the weights and cut the chords. As the man regained his breath, the robber snapped his large whip and said, "You are now my slave." Again he cracked his whip and told the man to move along.

Every day the robber had this man at work, cracking his whip. Like an ox he plowed fields, like a horse he carried the robber on his shoulders; he spent some days gathering fruit from the orchards, and on others he spent counting out the thief's treasure.

At first all this work was a joy in contrast to the crushing weights of the first robber. However, soon days began to merge in each other and his back strained under his labors, and silently the man prayed for freedom at each crack of the whip.

Finally, when he was lying exhausted in a moment of reprieve, his master off tending to some other affair, the robber in white came and said to him, "Traveler, do you seek freedom? Then come with me."

Calmly the third robber led the man throughout the forest. He said little if anything at all, though he smilingly pointed at some of the marvels on the way. Occasionally, the robber would burst out in songs about God or recite sacred poems. Often he just smiled and held the traveler's hand. In the presence of this robber the traveler soon lost his fatigue. Finally they came to a road.

"This is the road to the kingdom from which you came," said the robber in white.

"Come with me, friend," said the traveler. "You will be well rewarded for your service in freeing me."

The robber smiled. "I cannot, for I am a thief. I was born one and will always be so."

Yama and I, still as crows, watched the man go forth upon the road while his liberator returned back into the forest.

****

When we transformed back into the shapes of men we stopped alone on the road.

"Okay, no doubt there is hidden meaning in this past scene," I said. "Who was the traveler and who were the robbers?"

"The traveler is the self or the individual, the I sense of consciousness that identifies with a body—whether physical or metaphysical.

"The thieves are the qualities found everywhere in the Universe, for they are the qualities of the mind.

"The first, the Black, is named Tamas, or ignorance.

"He is a dullard, a sloth, paralyzed by fear; he is the eater of unclean flesh and food decaying. To be in his power is to sink into the squalor of despair. And death is the only release. Or so Tamas says.

43

"However the second thief, named Rajas or Passion, the Red one, can free one from the darkness by his passions, his fire. Just as fire can free water trapped in ice. Out of the dullness of inactivity he whips the individual into action, like a storm blowing a stagnant lake into a lake of waves, and dispersing the slime.

"Deeds are done, goals are accomplished, the feeling of 'I am getting something done' warms the soul.

"Yet Rajas does not stop with his whip.

"With every desire fulfilled a hundred more seeds are strewn in the field of the mind.

"Hopes of gain and fear of losing occupies the thoughts of Rajas.

"What was freedom for the soul or individual becomes enslavement. "And the soul cries for release.

"Thus hearing the soul's cry for release, Sattwa the pure, the White one, comes and frees the soul from the whip of Rajas by gently leading him into the beauty of nature, the appreciation of the sacred and to hear the silence within one's Self, just as the sun calmly and steadily shines its rays upon the lake, freeing the water from the earth to rise into the sky."

"The road Sattwa leads one upon is the road of virtues. The individual becomes calm as he knows he nears his Origin.

"However, being that Sattwa is of the mind, of nature, of all that is manifest, it is still a robber; he cannot go to the Origin of the soul, to That which Is beyond the mind.

"Thus," concluded Yama, "while the mind can point to liberation, it is powerless to take one there."

"Why are they called robbers, these qualities of the mind?" I asked.

"These three are thieves because being of the mind, the soul's Awareness of the original state of Oneness is stolen, and the soul identifies itself with the manifested, forgetting the Unity, and believes itself separate.

"Only when the mind of one is taught that no happiness lies in the world of changing forms, and that by only finding the Eternal Being can happiness be found, then the mind points the soul, the individual, back home."

Chapter XI
Satisfying desires; sex; guilt; self control;the naked body's symbolism

"Thank you, Yama," I said, "you have shown clearly that by fostering virtues the mind leads one to liberation; yet, in themselves are not the goal. Tell me, please, is it virtuous to abstain from sex? Some say it is as natural as eating, and like eating should be done in moderation."

"Only the ignorant would say such a thing, those who continue to seek to taste the sweet fruits of the world, while hoping to avoid the bitter. Yet I as death exist in both. "One eats to feed the body, that the soul may find freedom in one's life as a human being. And one ought to eat in moderation. "One needs to copulate to create bodies for other souls needing a human body to find freedom.

"Yes, one can express love-which certainly leads one into the expansion of unity-through having sex, just as one can express

45

love by the cooking and sharing of a meal. Yet if one is really wanting to share love, and not in truth just seeking pleasure, love is not restricted to having sex.

"Behold that child."

In front of us ran a naked little boy chasing a hoop. The hoop rolled into some bushes. Heedless he ran into them to retrieve the hoop.

"Isn't that poison oak?" I asked Yama.

"It certainly is."

He took the hoop out and off he went chasing it some more.

"He is totally unaware of his body, his nakedness," he said. "However soon, poisoned by the bush, he will think of nothing else but to satisfy his body's need to be scratched.

"And once he starts scratching he will not be able to stop until scratching becomes painful as his body oozes with sores.

"And so it is with sex. If youth is not protected from the lures of the pleasures of sex, which is so pervasive in your society, not guided to the Goal beyond the body and the mind, the hoop, then once he starts he will itch and itch, and will become little more than a rutting beast, seeing other human beings as nothing more than bodies needing to satisfy his itch."

"I understand what you say, dear Yama; yet what happens to one who was not protected and has scratched over many years?" I asked a little sheepishly, trying hard not to scratch the itches that were popping up over my body.

"Can the itching stop?"

"Yes it can stop; yet not without effort. However, just like any virtue it is not the goal, but can help one achieve the goal.

"The mind must be drawn away from the world and focused on the divine, whether with form, like a god or goddess, or without form, as in the Light of Consciousness.

"One can control one's breath, associate with the holy, read scriptures and engage the body in healthy physical activities.

"And, of course," he said, laughing, "take plenty of cold showers!"

"Should one feel guilty when one scratches that powerful itch?"

Yama laughed even louder.

46

"Guilt will always keep you bound to this world; for guilt tells you that you are not divine, that you are a little speck in the cosmos called your body, that you must get someplace called perfection in order to be divine

."No, guilt does not help; but awareness and truthfulness does. When you scratch do not pretend you are not or make up some excuse why you must. Scratch and give it to God. And then like with all activity let God take care of it."

****

"See those two monks over there by the river?" asked Yama.

"Yes. One of them is helping a young lady cross it by carrying her."

"He certainly is. Look at the other monk."

"He looks quite angry," I said.

Yama said nothing. I watched the one carrying the lady across the deep waters and then set her down. With a calm face he headed our way. The other monk fumed, his face twisted in contortions.

When they reached us the monk who had carried the woman bowed to Yama while the other seemed not to have even noticed us. Without being able to contain it any longer the latter blurted out:

"You touched a woman! You are a monk! Not only did you touch her, but you carried her. And you were happy the whole while!"

The calm monk looked at us and then asked me, "Who has carried the woman longer? He or I?"

The other monk looked puzzled. For a moment I did not know what to say, for obviously only this monk had carried the woman. Then when I saw Yama with his big grin I realized the monk's point and all three of us broke out in laughter. The serious monk turned red at being the butt of a joke he did not understand.

I said to him, "Dear monk, your brother let go of the woman at the river. But you have carried her in your mind from the moment he touched her."

The calm monk bowed to us and off they went, the other silent and sullen, stood there still carrying the woman.

47

"That is dwelling upon an act," said Yama as he continued his lesson.

"Resist what you can, for as long as you can; however do not overly strain. The more self-control, the more grace can help you.

"And the more Grace the more self-control.

"When you become free from itching I, as death, will not chase after you.

"In each body there are stored vital forces that keep the mind strong and the body healthy. The man can lose his vital forces with each ejaculation, dispersing them into the world.

"Instead this force could be directed, like a laser, to the divine. The sexual urge is more difficult, more obvious for a man. Many a great man has fallen to the baseness of sex.

"Women do not lose their vital forces like men losing their semen, yet they can become attached to the pleasure. Also as they take in a man's life force, they take in some of his qualities as well.

"Now not only does the woman have to overcome her own lower tendencies but has acquired new ones as well."

"Please tell me more about sex, Yama, since it entices so many in the world."

"The human body can be viewed as a beautiful book of knowledge, or a divine form of creation, instead of a means to gratify the desire for pleasures.

"A man's sexual organ, located in the area of the will, is external, reminding him that he is to act in the world with one-pointed attention.

"His organ points upward when aroused reminding him his greatest arousal lies in acting for higher purposes.

"The woman, on the other hand, has her sexual organs inside. Her actions are greatest on the whole inwardly, passively, taking in the active forces of creation, to gestate into wisdom.

"Her outward-ness comes in expressing her love, as her breasts extend outward from her heart area. She is the natural nurturer and she derives true pleasure from nurturing. "For in

48

nurturing, giving, she will find the expression of love and reminds others of their divinity.

"The man, however, finds love not outwardly so much but inwardly. His real breasts are on the inside suckling his own divinity; which then grows into action in the world.

"This is why men generally seek solitude to find themselves while women generally need to be with others."

Tell me, dear Yama," I said, "there are many in my land who speak of the path of Tantra, which may involve sexual rituals among other things. Can one be liberated, find the Self through such actions?"

Yama smiled. "Remember, no action can bring one home. What you speak of is one aspect of Tantra, called the Left-Handed Path, which espouses transforming desires and directing them towards the divine. Unlike the cultivation of virtues of the Right-Handed Path, virtues are not emphasized or sometimes eschewed outright with the left-handed one. Powers are sought by harnessing the fire of sexual energies and the mind. "It is wrought with dangers. The practitioner must keep her focus on the divine, otherwise powers will entrap her.

"In your time, in your culture of the West, many are taking pieces of various puzzles, pathways, and trying to make them fit.

"Many are walking one moment on the right path, then their minds or some book, tell them to spiritualize their desires and fulfill them, thereby sending them to the left path.

"And so they become jugglers, constantly picking up the balls they drop, going nowhere.

"Either follow one side or the other. But mind you, the right side is safer.

"Of course, better yet, is the No-Path, or the Pathless Path; but few want that one."

Chapter XII
The Pathless Path; remembering what is already there

"Why does no one want the No-Path?" I asked. "And please tell me what that path is or, I guess you might say, is not."

"Few are interested in the Pathless Path because their minds are their masters. The mind finds nothing interesting in it, nothing to overcome, nothing to acquire, nothing to flee from.

"It is a boring story for the mind. It makes no sense for it because no time is involved, no steps to be walked.

"And time is nothing but the mind.

"See that group of men over there about ready to cross the river?"

"Yes."

"How many are there?"

"There are ten men," I answered.

"Watch."

The ten men waded through the high waters in a single line, worry playing upon their faces at the possibility of being swept away. However, they persevered and soon they stood dripping wet on the other side. They huddled in a group.

"Are we all here?" one of them asked. He began counting heads, pointing to all the heads he saw.

"Oh no! One of us is missing!"

Someone else frantically began to count heads.

"Sure enough, one of us is missing!"

All of them desperately counted each other.

"Where is the missing one!" they all shouted as they ran and stumbled along the riverbank searching for the one being swept down the river.

Then a man with a serene face came out of the forest in response to their cries.

"Fellows, why are you shouting? Why all this frantic actions and worried looks?" the stranger inquired.

"Why?! One of us is lost, no doubt swept away down the river.

One is lost, eh? How many of you set out crossing the river?"

"Ten."

"And how many did you count who had made it over?"

"We all counted nine."

The man raised his eyebrows and counted aloud very deliberately. And he counted ten heads.

"No one is missing. You are whole"

"Can it be true?" they asked incredulously. "Do count again lest you counted wrongly."

And so once more the man counted aloud and deliberately.

"Ten."

"How wonderful! Thank you, you have saved us! You have made us whole!"

They all bowed at the stranger's feet.

The man laughed. "I have done nothing. None of you counted yourself. I have only pointed out what has always been.

"No one was lost. Nor was there ever anyone missing."

****

"Is that it?" I asked Yama after we watched the man, shaking his head in disbelief, leave the ten men as they jumped up and down embracing one another, and disappear into the forest.

"I am not sure of the lesson, besides the fact that not everyone is dished out with the same amount of wits."

Silently Yama walked down a path that turned into a road through a noisy, bustling marketplace. I knew by now that his silence meant that he would be showing me the answer to my question. We entered a shop full of glittering jewelry. A man sat behind a table.

"Goldsmith," Yama said to the man, "take this gold and fashion a wonderful ring out of it."

Yama handed him a large golden nugget and immediately the goldsmith went to work, melting, pounding, shaping, polishing. After a while, he held up a magnificent ring.

Yama showed it to me.

"Do you remember the gold nugget?"

"Certainly."

"Has it changed?"

"Of course," I said. "It began as a clump of gold and by his skill the goldsmith has created a ring."

"True enough. Yet what about the gold-ness of the nugget, has it changed?

"Is the gold any less by the changing of its shape—from the beginning through to the end?"

"No," I said excitedly, beginning to get his point. "It is still gold no matter what form, what shape!"

"Yes," said Yama, "that is the Pathless Path. It is simply remembering your Essence.

"Remembering That which has never changed no matter what forms you have appeared to be in, or in whatever action.

"For like the ten travelers realizing no one was lost in the first place, that there is no one to look for and no time for which to be found."

"Is it that simple? Then why all the scriptures and religions and practices?"

Yama gently tapped a finger on my chest.

"Because it is so simple. The Answer lies ever shining right here, waiting right in the heart.

However, people believe they are their minds, and the mind loves stories and schemes and strategies.

"And since most are dictated by their minds it is not easy to always remember your Essence when you walk amongst the busy-minded crowd.

"That is why it is important for being in holy company, to sit in the silence of truth, with those who remember and who can remind you by counting your head."

Chapter XIII
What is Real? The beginning of the dream; changing scenery

With his words seeping into my heart like rain being sucked into the dry earth, we silently walked through the market place. Contemplating his words I closed my eyes a moment, and when I opened them we stood by a pool where a waterfall gently fell.

I shook my head in amazement at how quickly scenes would change traveling with Yama.

"Yama, you who are leading me back to my Origin," I said, finding myself a moss-covered boulder to sit upon, "this is a dream, yes?"

"Yes."

"When I wake up will that also be a dream? Is one more real than the other? Is any of it real at all? My mind cannot fathom these questions and is confused; yet strangely I feel calm with an inner certainty."

"How many scriptures and philosophies have tried to adequately answer your questions. Let me now try.

"Neither your waking nor your dreaming are real; although while your consciousness is dwelling in either state you will believe that state to be real and that the other is not. Yet even as both are equally unreal, they are both real as well. "And they are neither unreal nor real."

"Excuse me," I said, my face twisting once again with paradoxes, "your statements cancel one another. Thus you have said nothing."

"True. I have said nothing to answer your questions beyond a doubt because really your questions cannot be answered beyond a doubt. The problem is that you believe you are the questioner and that there is an answer.

"Question and answer. Subject and object. The dreamer and the dream.

"Is the world real or not? Is God and the world one?

"All these questions cannot be answered satisfactorily—that is, going beyond the shadows of doubt to rest in the Still Place of knowing—because they originate in the world of duality.

"The Answer is only found in the Silence of Knowing which is beyond the duality of words.

"For when you go into the silence there is no more questioner. There never was, nor will there ever be.

"There is only certainty of Being.

"Remember, it is the mind's activity to question and to figure out things, and no activity can lead to the truth."

I put my hands on my head trying to stop it from spinning away. Yama laughed.

"Let me tell you a story.

"A long time ago, before time began and space was created, Brahman fell asleep and dreamt he did not know himself. A question arose: 'Who am I?'

"And from that question time arose to allow time for the answer to be found and space arose to offer an arena in which to seek the answer.

"An unlimited expression of forms were created by the Mind of Brahman in an attempt to discover his own vastness.

"And for countless ages Brahman watched within himself the answers to this question. And being that Brahman is unlimited in his vastness, and that the universe was created in order for the answer to be explored, the question forever goes on and on and on."

I nodded in understanding.

"The problem is," Yama continued, "is that Brahman, who is the Eternally Awakened One, the Omniscient One, could never fall asleep nor could he ever not know."

I groaned as once again the paradoxes sped around the track of my mind. With my mind threatening to shatter; it simply shut down. And for a long while I sat in silence.

****

I came out of the silence feeling refreshed and said, "I realize the mind cannot figure out the Answer, yet how does one stay in the Awareness of Knowing?"

As soon as I asked the question an old hermit of a man came up to me and shook his staff.

55

"If you want the answer you must leave the city and all its lures, its desires. You will only find it here in the wilderness."

Then off he went, disappearing into the woods. Just as I was ready to make comment to Yama about the old man, a man in a business suit approached.

"Ignore the old man," said the businessman. "The city is not the problem."

And off he went as well, yet going in the opposite direction, following the road.

Yama looked at me and asked which one of the two men did I think spoke correctly.

"I would imagine the hermit," I replied.

"Why do you say so? Is it that he looks the part of a holy man? Be aware of appearances. A deadly coral snake resembles the benign milk snake."

"You mean to tell me that the business man was the holy man? But the hermit has given up all of the world to find God."

Yama shook his head. He reached down and grabbed a shovel that had just manifested, and began digging where his shadow lay.

I watched perplexed as the hole grew; sweat poured down Yama's brow.

"What are you doing, may I ask?"

Without stopping his digging he replied: "I am burying my shadow, naturally."

"That's ridiculous. No one can bury their shadow!"

Yama threw down the shovel and stood wiping the sweat.

"Exactly.

"Renouncing the world, family, work, riches, etc., and going off into the wilderness to become holy is no different than trying to bury your shadow.

"You take your mind wherever you may go.

"That holy-looking hermit had a mind filled with thoughts of the upturned breasts of a young maiden bathing down the river he had passed; while the businessman silently blessed everyone he saw by saying: 'You are That.'"

"Do you mean, dear teacher, that going out into the wild, away from distractions of the city, is not beneficial for one's growth?"

"Certainly not," Yama replied. "I highly recommend going out in nature alone, for a day or for longer periods. I find people's minds tend to quiet down after three days. It is like a fast from city life.

"However, the growth that you speak of really has nothing to do with becoming aware of who you are, the One who is unchanging, beyond growth.

"And that the great inquiry can be done anywhere and at all times."

"What do you mean by inquiry?" I asked.

"Ahh, that is what the Sage sitting in the hall teaches. It is the inquiry that leads all beyond my grasp."

Chapter XIV
The great inquiry; beyond definitions; digging out the thorn; the battle; the teacher; mantras

Yama said, "Do you remember the question that Brahman asked when he started to dream?"

"Yes. Who am I?"

"And what happened then?"

"Everything became created."

"Yes, time began. And when there exists time, there I also exist as death. The great inquiry, or Self-inquiry, is the vehicle in which to go beyond time."

"Please, dear Yama, explain the method of Self-inquiry that the Sage speaks of."

"Very well, listen carefully.

"It is the most subtle of teachings. There is no fat for which to chew upon, no games to get distracted in. Few can follow it to its destination.

"If you take hold of it no longer will I need to be your teacher and this dream ends. If not, well, the dream and more questions and more answers will continue.

"The mind tells you constantly who you are by having you focus on some problem the mind brings to you. For instance, the mind will play over and over again an argument you might have had with your wife, what was said, what you should have said, what you would liked to have said. All of which have the underlining definition that you are the husband of your wife, with an added good husband or bad husband pending on your actions.

"Of course, this is not the only underlining definition you'll be unconsciously identifying your Self with.

"Wherever there exists a stress, a worry, fear, anxiety, repeated planning and review, the Self becomes forgotten and the mind has wrapped you in a definition."

"You mean," I said, "that if I worry about my son's progress in school, I am believing I am his father? Or if I am worried about the stock market crashing and the loss of my wealth, I am identifying my Self as a rich man?"

"Yes. And you remember that any definition, any Self-identification with any role, traps you in time.

"Thus the Self-inquiry of the Sage is to stop the mind immediately when it begins to ramble. As soon as a thought arises—any thought, whether great or trivial—you are to ask the question: "To whom does this thought arise?

"Now if you let the mind answer the question you would receive all kinds of answers, so many definitions. That is why you do not let the mind run away with answering, and instead answer: "To me. Who am I?

"Again the mind will try to give all kinds of answers by bringing up all kinds of thoughts. Yet as soon as a thought arises you repeat: "To whom does this thought come? To me. Who am I?'

"Constantly you must keep vigilant, watching that trickster of the mind.

"Until the mind gives up the stories and the unbounded silence is the Answer."

"Throughout the day one must keep up the inquiry?" I asked. "Even when working on a problem, for instance doing math or being a lawyer and working on a case?"

"If the mind is rightfully engaged in a task at hand then the mind is doing its work. It is serving by the use of its intelligence. And if you are established in the Self the mind works properly, automatically.

"Generally, for most of the day, you will be doing one thing while the mind is straying elsewhere, as into the future, the past or to some fantasy."

Yama gave me a hard stare with the last word, and I could feel the heat fill my face. Oh yes, I have definitely had my fill of fantasies.

"These become the times when the mind seduces, opening itself wide with all kinds of images. Immediately do the inquiry before the mind strings you along too far."

"Just a minute. You say the mind is a trickster. Yet isn't the mind being used for Self-inquiry?" I asked.

"Yes, you are making the mind work for you and not you working for the mind.

"See this?"

****

Yama showed me the palm of his hand. A large thorn stood deeply embedded in his palm, In his other hand he held an identical thorn.

"The thorn is the mind. For most people they exist impaled by the mind and suffer daily."

"Yet if you asked most people," I interjected, "well, at least those who live well off materially, they would not say that they suffered from their minds. They probably would tell you that their minds got them to their high standing."

"True, because they do not want to look at the thorn. The pain that the thorn inflicts is called normal by the thorn.

"I am supposed to be here, the thorn says, that is part of life. Sure there exists a little pain, but the pleasures I can get you—if you keep me in—will make you forget the pain.

"Yet for the wise one, who possesses no fear to look upon the thorn, who tires of living in suffering, who realizes how fleeting and deceptive are pleasures, he desires nothing more than to remove the thorn."

With the thorn Yama held he began to dig out the embedded one. And after a little grimacing (no doubt for my benefit) and a little blood, the thorn came free.

"The wise," continued Yama, "takes the mind firmly in hand and uses it to remove itself."

"What about the grimacing and the blood? It looks painful," I asked.

"I will not lie to you and say it is easy; for the mind is barbed and deeply embedded.

"When you begin to dig you will find all sorts of thoughts, definitions and stories buried inside. You might see thoughts that you would have only associated with the most despicable of the world, and the mind will whisper: See what you are?

"And it only gets worse if you keep digging.

"However not only horrid thoughts will you uncover, like curses waiting for a grave robber to take revenge upon, you may also release thoughts of such immense beauty or genius that you would only have associated with the greatest figures. "And the mind will whisper:

"Yes, that's right, you too stand with the great ones. Enjoy the glory, do great things. No need to dig any further.

"Thus one grimaces at seeing such horrible things, then one grimaces at letting go of those wonderful thoughts."

"And the blood?" I asked.

"The blood is the battle. The mind does not want to let go of its position of authority.

"Here, let me show you this war. Brace yourself; it will not be pleasant."

If Yama warned that what lay ahead might not be pleasant, I braced myself.

61

****

In his way, the way of dreams, the scenery changed. We stood in a muddy trench, the stench of death everywhere. Next to us crouched wide-eyed soldiers wearing what I recognized were World War I uniforms. And then I realized so did we, only our uniforms were those of officers.

"What?" I began to stutter before Yama ducked down, pulling me with him.

"Get ready," he said excitedly. "They're charging!"

A trumpet blew and a yell from across the field shattered the silence. The men to either side of us began to fire rifles and machine guns.

"What do I do?" I yelled.

"Just shoot the machine gun and I will feed you the bullets."

I began shooting slowly, scrutinizing all the charging soldiers individually and shooting only the ones who looked the meanest or the ugliest.

Yet doing so, many of the attacking soldiers jumped into our trench and bayoneted our men.

"Stop looking at them like that. Who cares if some of them are pleasant to look at?" Yama yelled over the noise of battle. "Both will kill us. Just shoot!"

And so I did. I mowed them down all over the bloody field, until nothing moved at all, my gun glowing red.

I slumped down on the side of the trench, exhausted.

Suddenly several enemy soldiers jumped into our trench and began shooting and impaling our soldiers. Yama cut them down with his sword.

"Keep vigilant!" he shouted at me between sword blows.

"I looked over the side and saw the whole field covered with the charging enemy, as many as before. On and on I kept firing, Yama now holding the bullet belt as he fed my machine gun. At last all lay dead.

"Keep vigilant," he warned.

Sure enough pockets of the enemy rose out of their trench. However, if I kept vigilant and shot them as they struggled out of their trench, I found keeping them back much easier and less tiring.

My weapon did not overheat either. After a while an occasional soldier would pop up his head, and I quickly dispatched him.

Until no soldiers came out at all. A great cheer erupted from our side. Victory! We had won!

"Look!" cried one of our men.

What looked like a general and a group of handsome officers approached, waving a white flag.

"Shoot them! Yama cried. "Shoot them now!"

"Yama, I can't shoot them. They're holding a flag of truce."

"You'll be sorry," Yama said under his breath as I told some men to bring the officers here.

The general and his men spoke our language perfectly and acted very affably. They said they were mine to command as I seemed to be the ranking officer of my side. I had them clear the dead and begin cleaning our trenches out. I had some of my men watch them while others I had guarding the front lest there might be some surprise attack.

"There exists no more of my men, I can reassure you," said the general to me as he noticed what I was doing.

"Your scouts have seen no enemy. Let us help make this a better place so we can all enjoy it here and relax. To live in peace and fight no more."

Since no enemy seemed to be left anymore I let the general bring forth some ideas. Soon, instead of mud trenches my men and his officers built wooden sides and floors. They even made some nice quarters to sleep in. He taught us exercises to keep us fit; he started a chess tournament to sharpen our wits and created a choir to keep up our spirits.

At first I still maintained guards to monitor the front, but after getting to know these fine fellows and hearing their promises that the war was over, I let everyone join in. We all became very happy together.

All the while, Yama kept a stern visage about him. So immersed I had become in this drama I had completely forgotten why we had come here in the first place, and I began to see Yama as not my teacher but as an officer of a lower rank. I would even call him a kill-joy at times, at which he replied with only the lifting of his eye brows.

And then it happened. Night had fallen and guards stood watch. Then yells shattered the night and a host of the enemy charged amongst us, slashing with bayonets. My men fell everywhere. We stood defenseless. I saw the general and the other officers gleefully hacking up my men. All my men lay dead and the general rushed at me.

All I could do was to yell for Yama. The trench in front of me exploded in a roar and a flash. All of the enemy lay dead when the smoke cleared.

Yama walked up to me, hand grenades with strange letters strapped about his chest.

"Get to your post!" he commanded. "The war is not over."

Hundreds of the enemy came screaming at us. I shot the machine gun while he threw his bombs. Throughout the night we fought until silence met us in the morning.

****

"Have you learned anything from all this?" he asked."

To listen to you?" I said sheepishly, exhausted from the battle.

"To listen to one's teacher is wise, true. Then again, this lesson would not have followed if you had listened to me in the first place.

"What I meant by the question was why this battle? Why did we fight in the first place?"

The exhaustion from the fight had made my brain feel frozen in place. I just stared at him speechless awhile.

"It was about the blood when you pulled out the thorn," I managed to say as I looked around at all the bloody corpses.

"Yes, you have now witnessed and participated in the war of the mind.

"The embedded thorn was the enemy and the freeing thorn was our side. The machine gun you manned was Self-inquiry and you were shooting down the thoughts the mind sent to overwhelm you.

"What happened when you picked and chose the enemy, those thoughts?"

64

"I could not pick and choose without allowing many to reach our trench," I answered.

"So what did you do then?"

"I just shot anyone who moved, which proved far more successful."

"And thus it is with Self-inquiry. Every thought must be shot down. And as soon as they arise, or the field will soon be swarming with thoughts before you know what has happened.

"How was your attitude through the battle?" Yama continued.

"I was intense. I fought for my life as well as for the others."

"You should do Self-inquiry with the same intensity; for you are fighting for real freedom, for your life."

"Throughout the whole day I should be shooting down all rising thoughts?" I asked. "It seems exhausting."

"Shoot down every thought, especially during those times with eyes closed that are set aside daily for Self-inquiry.

"And as you become more proficient during those times, do it here and there throughout the day, until every moment—except when the mind is serving to accomplish a task—you are shooting down every thought.

"For if you try to man the gun for the whole day right away, like the gun, your brain will overheat and you will give up the practice.

"What is most important is that you do the Self-inquiry with intensity, because finding the Answer of who you are is the greatest accomplishment; while, at the same time needing to be as calm as I was in the trenches due to the knowing that you are already the Answer, and that there is nothing to lose."

****

"Do you want to know the greatest secret?" Yama looked intently at me.

"Yes, dear teacher, please tell the greatest secret."

"Knowing who you are is the only reason you have an earthly body—unless, you are one of the ones who return to remind deluded minds about who they are. That is why the inquiry is all important."

"Because I did not shoot down everyone as you had instructed me to do—for instance, the general and his men—that was my big mistake, yes?" I asked, starting to grasp what Yama was teaching and digesting the experience.

"Correct. When you set out to do Self-inquiry, to dive into the reason for being, no quarter can be given, no matter how pleasing the thought is. "Because once you let in a thought, it will put you off guard by diverting your attention from Self-inquiry, and will get you engaged in all kinds of distractions.

"Once you have been infiltrated by the out-going mind, you are in its power, and all the forces of the mind will come pouring forth.

"And the quest becomes long forgotten."

"Yes, I think I understand. For by allowing the mind in and allowing it to move about, without any vigilance on my part, by the time it attacked again to reclaim its control, I could not even do Self-inquiry.

"All I could do was cry for help."

"And so your teacher came.

"Remember that. Because truth wants to be known and that I am one with Truth, Truth sent me.

"The truth of who you are will always send some form to help you when you cry out.

"The true Guru always hears the devotee's call."

"What were the bombs you threw, those ones with the strange-looking writing upon them?" I asked.

"Mantras or incantations, you might say. They can be most effective in subduing the mind, or quieting it.

"When Self-inquiry becomes too difficult, with the mind swirling around like a tempest, use mantras, especially those given by one who abides in the Self."

****

We sat in the silence awhile. I chewed over his words and reviewed my experience.

"When I manned the machine gun, or did Self-inquiry, I could only do it a short time alone; otherwise, I would run out of bullets," I said.

"That's true."

"You were needed to help me."

"Correct."

"Well, what does that mean in the daily use of Self-inquiry?" I asked.

"My help was the grace of the Guru, of the Self, of God, whatever you may want to say.

"By your effort you received grace.

"And by grace you could continue to do your effort."

"Is a guru necessary for finding the truth?"

"In the beginning you can go fairly far without a guru; but soon you will reach a dead end. Then an outer teacher is needed.

"Why an outer, you might ask? Because you believe you are a form and a personality. So you can really only identify with the Truth as having a form and a personality.

"Then this outer one will lead you to the true Guru—the I AM that abides within.

"It is said that when a man is guided by himself he is guided by a fool. Few are guided by the Self and the mind is a trickster that is not easily subdued."

We sat some more in the trench, looking out at the quiet field. New men had replaced the fallen ones on our side, removing the dead bodies from the trench.

"This quiet is very peaceful," I said.

"I could stay forever in it."

"Yes' it is peaceful. But it's not the true Peace of the Self. It is only peaceful in contrast to the war with the mind.

"With any contrast there exists duality. And to find your Self, which is the One Self of All, there cannot be two.

"Close your eyes; I want to show you something."

JANAKA

Chapter XV
The illusion of trance; the false guru; all are teachers; the lure of being special; powers

I saw a man dressed like a yogi. He sat by a river. A disciple came to him just as he readied himself for meditation and asked if there was anything he could get for him. The yogi replied that he was thirsty and told the other to fetch some water from the river. He then slipped into meditation.

A hundred years passed. Vines grew over the yogi's body. The river shifted its course and flowed faraway. When the yogi came out, he cried out for water.

The vision ended and I opened my eyes.

"Please explain what I beheld," I asked Yama.

"The yogi you saw, by subduing the mind, put himself into a peaceful state of mind, much like sitting in this quiet field.

"If you only silence the mind, any desire, any thought patterns that have not been dispelled, will come out sooner or later. They are still part of the thorn."

"His thirst was such a desire?" I said.

"Yes, and it matters not how long one is in this quiet or trance-like state, the desires will still be there upon coming out; just as when one goes to sleep at night and experiences the peace of deep sleep. The next morning, regardless of how peaceful, the same tendencies and desires will be waiting."

"How to avoid this trance?" I asked. "How do you know when you are in it and not in the true peace of the Self?"

Yama replied: "Only when both armies are gone will you have true peace. "In other words when there is no longer a questioner who can ask: Who is it that beholds this peace, this quiet?

"When there exists no I to behold the peace. When no one exists to raise the question or to give the answer, then true peace of the Self will arise.

"So to avoid that trance of false peace you must continue the inquiry: "Who is experiencing this peace?

"I am.

"Who am I?

"As long as there is one to observe anything the inquiry must continue. Until only Being remains."

"Yama," I said, "it seems impossible to keep up the vigilance. The world is so alluring, filled with endless enticements. And the path of inquiry seems very lonely as everything must be cut away."

"Yes it seems impossible; but impossible only to the mind that wants to be in charge.

"You must ask yourself if the one who sees Self-inquiry as impossible is your true infinite, all-knowing, all-powerful Self or the false self of limited ideas of definitions?"

"It must be the false self," I replied.

"Good. When you listen to such doubts you heed a lie. Cut away the lie and dive into the inquiry.

"And your statement about being alone? Remember who fed the machine gun?"

"You did."

"Correct, your teacher that the Self sent to you. You cannot do this alone. The Master is always with you."

"How does one find a Guru? Sure there are plenty of gurus out there. However, I mean a true Guru, one who is established in the Self?" I asked.

"Did you find me or did I find you? Or both and neither?"

"Well I was not looking for you—at least not consciously. Yet I long for the truth of life and death. I don't know if you were looking for me, for you just showed up; and in quite a dramatic way, I might add."

Yama bowed.

"It does seem like it just happened. I do not know. It seems all so very mysterious," I continued.

"It is mysterious. The Master and disciple is the greatest of the mysteries of the Great Mystery. For which one creates the other? It is the last illusion of separation, the last step before unity of the Self.

"For the Guru sees no disciple. He sees only the Self. While the disciple is pushed inward by the Guru only to discover the Guru is pulling him down from the inside."

"Okay," I said, "yet how does one know if the teacher he comes to is the Guru, is a true master? What if you choose wrongly?"

"Everyone you meet is a teacher; there is always something to learn from any relationship, no matter how brief or how long the relationship might last. "Can you love them as they are? Do they repulse you? Why do they repulse you? Or do they attract you and why?

"Everyone can teach you about yourself.

"However, there are some who stand in the position of teachers. "For example ... .

****

I found myself walking through the doors of a metaphysical bookstore. Yama was nowhere to be seen. Behind the counter sat two men. One of them was rather pudgy with intense eyes behind thick plastic rimmed glasses.

"So you have come," the pudgy man said. "It is good to see you again. So good."

Again? I had never seen him before; however, I was drawn to him and sat down in the chair he beckoned me towards. He waved his hand and a large mineral appeared.

"This is for you."

"Thanks" I muttered, not certain about what I had just seen.

The other man said that he was picking up in the Cosmic Records that I was some famous person, and the other agreed and named who I had been along with even more amazing historical figures. I might as well have been told I was Napoleon or Cleopatra.

I felt a rush of fascination. Maybe it's true? Maybe I was those people? When they invited me to their land out in the desert I jumped at the chance. Could this be my Master? I thought. There is such a pull.

The first few days I lived in heaven. The man with the glasses materialized gems for me, would touch me and send me into a bliss undreamt of, read my mind and explained my past and foretold my future, called down spaceships for me to see, and told me I was his son and that he was the Only Begotten Son of God.

Oh, how special I felt; how special the twelve of us were who served this master. He called us the elite of God, created by God in a special way to lead souls back to God and to prepare for the earth changes and the New World.

71

Then the days turned to hell as this teacher made mudras (hand movements) and an etheric fire would burn upon my neck with an agonizing force, demanding my total surrender to his will. Other times wrathful spirits would manifest through him, changing his face into fearful distortions, and I watched in horror and dismay this teacher strangle willful disciples. I saw struggling disciples lifted off the ground by their necks who refused to do his bidding.

"You are either with me or against me. If you are against me you are against God. And God will cast you out into the far reaches of space, into the nether worlds."

I fled into the desert. I prayed and prayed to be able to surrender to him, who surely was my Guru. He certainly must be my master, for that drawing to be with him, to love him, I have felt with no other person. And who else would have such powers?

Yet...yet...how could God cast me out? How could I get outside of God Who exists everywhere?

Wait a minute, I said to myself, feeling a growing rage, this is not the truth. I cannot be outside of God. God does not cast out. This is not my Guru. I do not choose to follow this path!

****

As I made this declaration, Yama appeared to me in the desert; a big grin upon his face.

"So you do not choose this path. Why?"

"He is not my teacher. He teaches lies!" I said angrily.

"He is not your teacher? Has he not taught you anything? Is there nothing positive you can bring forward into your future from this? Are there no warnings for your future as well? Or was it all just a big waste of time?

"And if it was a waste of time, and since I am time, then you would be saying that I really do not know what I am doing, that I am meaningless."

I did not want to hear this. I felt only anger. I felt betrayed, used. I had bared my soul to this man, who wanted to use me only for his own egotistical plans. I felt raped. I kept silent while Yama sat next to me. Neither of us said anything for a long while.

72

Finally, I regained my breath and the anger became replaced by more calm. And at last some words escaped from my tight jaws.

"By showing me the opposite path I came to realize without doubt that I cannot be outside of God."

"Good," replied Yama, "but why was this other path so alluring for you?"

I thought for a while.

"I was special. He told me about those famous people I might have been. And that I was among the chosen few of God and that we had a special mission."

Just thinking about it I could feel the warmth of excitement at the possibility that perhaps this teacher was really who he said he was, and that I may just be what he said I was. How glorious ... .

"Ahem!" Yama said, clearing his throat.

"Seductive isn't it? How do his new definitions for you, the elite of God, the son of the Son of God, harbingers of the New World, compare with the Infinite, Boundless Self?"

I shook my head vigorously, to shake out the deceptions.

"There is no comparison. His is a beautiful leaf decaying upon the floor of an endless forest of trees piercing the clouds."

"What else lured you?" he asked.

"Powers. Yes, powers. And I thought I was beyond craving powers. After all I denied what you offered so I may know the truth.

"Still, he displayed powers that I had wanted when I was a child—when I had had the fantasy of being a superhero."

"Once?"

"Well, perhaps I still may have that fantasy now and then."

"And what do you think those powers have done for him?"

"They have destroyed him," I said sadly, for I still felt a love for him.

"He has become deluded by them."

"Yes, the mind has awesome powers being that it is divinely created. It can do anything.

"If one has not found the Self that is beyond the mind, That which gives the mind its power, then when powers arise it is nearly impossible not to identify with those powers of the mind and not feel special.

73

"And that specialness is a cage that cuts you off from all creation.

"And since you feel cut off you will seek more power to feel expanded. However that only tightens the noose."

"Are all powers bad to possess?" I asked, a part of me hoping for some redeeming quality.

"If you want to go beyond my reach as death, just focus on having love for God and a desire for truth. And avoid seeking powers."

****

"Fine. Avoid powers and see that everyone is your teacher. Still," I said, "how does one know if he has found his true Guru, one who is established completely in the Self?"

"By outward appearances one cannot be known, as I have already demonstrated to you. Most likely you will be drawn by the peace you feel around this person. The true teacher abides in an all-pervasive peace. There is no need for dazzling tricks to lure you, no need for proclamations of being an avatar, bodhisattva, or such titles. Because the ready student has seen that nothing in the world can offer happiness and wants peace more than anything else.

"Let me tell you that few at anytime are embodied on the planet who could be called true Masters. It is no easy task to be rooted in the Self in this world."

"Those virtues you spoke about that need to be cultivated, are they to be found in the Guru, or is the Guru beyond them?"

"The Guru, and everyone in truth, are beyond the virtues; still while there appears to be two, of disciple and Guru, most likely the true Guru will have the virtues well established to set an example for the students to follow.

"While there exists few at any given time to be fully established in the Unmovable Self, many more, and many more to come as the world transitions into a more enlightened time, stand in a higher consciousness, so to speak.

"For such ones, little dirt or fewer negative tendencies remain to obstruct the reflection of the Self. It is most useful to seek their company for their vibrations can elevate your mind.

"Yet beware. They stand not firmly established beyond duality and tendencies may exist that may lead them and their followers downward if the students do not use the sword of discrimination and follow their own conscience."

"Does such a fall happen often?" I asked.

Yama smiled and shook his head. "Oh, how my wheel turns. Until one reaches the Immovable Hub of the Self, long will one rise and fall on the rim.

"Come, I want to show you a temple."

Chapter XVI
*The temple of consciousness; the serpents and angels; how
teachers fall; delusions of devotees*
76

I turned to follow Yama and saw a magnificent temple of seven stories. Just above the top of the roof shone a brilliant star in the middle.

"What is that?" I asked.

"Is it a star?"

"Let us call it the Light of Consciousness. It is the goal that each visitor to the temple must reach."

We walked through the iron gate on the ground level. An immense hallway, both wide and long stood before us. Others came after us through the door and moved towards the first group of people. As far as I could see I beheld various sized groups of people, all undressed.

"Who are these people entering through the gate in a countless stream?" I inquired.

"These are the players. They have come to play the game of hide-an-seek."

"For whom do they seek?"

"They seek the Self.

"Did you see any entering when we stood outside?"

"No, now that you mention it."

"We did not for we stood outside the arena of the Game. Yet now we stand in the first level; the level of Maya, illusion. The illusion that the One is many."

We began walking down past the groups. We passed one group. Flames burned all around them and curses flew from their mouths at each other. Now and then a giant serpent would appear and regurgitate a person onto this group in flames.

"Where are we?" I asked. "And what is that horrible snake?"

"We walk now through the realm of anger. And the snake just swallowed and regurgitated a person who stood high upon the seventh floor of the temple. He was a light upon the world, shining out as a beacon in the darkness.

"However, he was not careful and began to think that his individuality was the Light and the snake of egotism swallowed him.

"Now he has lost control and his anger at his falling from grace adds even more to this fire."

"Will he get out?"

"Oh, yes, and soon, for he has good habits that will lead him upward. People can live a lifetime or more on this first floor until they get tired of it. Or, as in most cases, in a day one can fall bitten by a serpent countless times and rise countless times."

We walked past a group where each person shoved huge amounts of food down their throats or sat on large piles of wealth.

"Greed?" I inquired.

Yama nodded. We walked this long hall past numerous groups, some playing in the mud, others building shelters and hunting for food and giving birth, others strutting around like peacocks looking in fascination at the mirrors before them; others copulating like animals. We came to a flight of stairs.

"This has been the physical plane of existence. No one will stay here because the game beckons them onward."

We climbed the stairs and entered a room where various people either fasted or kept long vigils, read scriptures or did penances.

"What are they doing?" I asked.

"They are purifying themselves after so long in body consciousness. We now stand on the astral level of consciousness, the plane where feelings dominate. These are going beyond their feelings, denying these emotions so that they may rise even into a higher plane."

All of a sudden an angelic being entered the room and took hold of a woman reading a holy book. Yama took my hand and we ascended after her. We arrived in a vast palace, where beings of wondrous splendor moved about.

"Where are we?" I asked.

"We are in what is called the celestial plane. Great beings reside here and go to those on the lower planes to help elevate them."

"It is like heaven," I said, looking around at this place of beauty and peace. I wanted to stay in this radiance forever. "Are we at the top?"

Yama laughed and said, "Yes, this is what people call heaven. But we are only on the third level."

"The third level? How could that be? What could be better than this?"

"Everyone who lives here still has the sense of individuality, no matter how pure. And with any sense of me-ness there is a you.

"There is God and I, the world and I. In other words, duality exists.

"And being not of Unity there still resides delusion.

"Watch this one and you will understand."

****

A saintly looking man, dressed in flowing white robes, garlands of flowers strung around his neck, sat cross-legged on a platform. Around him sat a group of devotees, adoration beaming out of their eyes. Some waved incense about him and most of them wore medallions around their necks with pictures of this man. They bathed in this holy man's radiance.

More and more followers came and sat at his feet, bowing, reaching out to perhaps touch his robe. With each new arrival the man's chest seemed to puff out the slightest bit, his chin rising a tad higher.

"Oi!" I heard Yama mutter behind me. "Here it comes."

Suddenly an enormous serpent rose up from the floor. No one, not even the holy man, noticed the immense snake. Then with a lightning-fast strike, the beast swallowed the holy man whole. Only a few in the crowd seemed to notice that the man had disappeared, and with disgust on their face, these few departed. The others, however, remained, looking with devoted eyes at the place where the man had sat, some even reaching out towards his imaginary gown.

"What happened?" I asked, shaken at what I saw, and confused by the devotees' response.

"I saw it coming. He chose to have around him a bunch of followers, those types that want to be told what to do with every aspect of their lives. They want to be 'devotees' and wear outrageous outfits and create a new movement or religion, in which they can climb upward in status, to be one of the inner circle.

"They desire neither love nor truth, only specialness. Each vie to have special attention from the light.

"And because he had that seed in him still, that tendency to be special, he attracted such a following. And so the bad company called forth the serpent of conceit and swallowed him down to the lower plane to the room of mirrors."

I watched one follower ask a question to the now empty spot, and saw him nod with understanding and bow with gratefulness as though he was given the answer.

"Why do these followers act as though nothing has happened?" I asked.

"It seems as though they see him still sitting in front of them."

"They act thus because they are not yet seeking truth, only grandiose definitions to wrap themselves into. Their new identities are blindfolds.

"They do not see their teacher for who he is, they see him as the symbol for what they want him to be.

"They want to be disciples of a savior, the new messiah, an avatar, not someone who still has human weaknesses. So they worship a lie and let the truth slip away."

****

We left them and traveled through many rooms and across many planes. The higher up in the temple the more magnificent beings I encountered, beings more like gods than humans, shining with the brilliance of suns. Throughout the halls I saw celestial beings carrying ones upward. Yet I also beheld enormous serpents swallowing countless of travelers, even those as splendid as the gods.

Up and up we went into the regions of light, feeling lighter and lighter.

"You have seen enough," Yama whispered.

"Time to leave the temple. We do not want to end the game too soon, do we?"

Chapter XVII
The paths of devotion and knowledge; giving up one's power

We sat in a run-down apartment, both of us wearing casual western clothes, the memory of the light of the upper regions still tingling my consciousness. Then I remembered the serpents.

And the serpents terrified me.

"Yama, you who lead every traveler through these halls, how can one reach the goal in that place; a place that seems no more than a temple of snakes? How to escape their ever-seeking tongues?"

"You ask me to reveal the greatest of secrets. Few have I given this answer. Yet you have asked me to be your teacher as well, and what kind of teacher would I be not to answer? Very well.

"There exists two paths to reach the goal and to escape the serpents. And in truth they are the same.

"One is to see the serpents as nothing else but God. And to see the celestial beings who bear one upwards as also but God.

"Only God exists.

"Think only of God. See only God. Accept all as God.

"Every room, every rise and fall is God. One plays the game only out of love for God, and enjoys rising because of God and falling because of God.

"Because rising and falling becomes the same, both being of God, duality ceases.

"There exists no more getting there. No more ups and downs. There becomes only here in God.

"This is the path of devotion. Its goal is certain. Love is the means and the end.

"The other is to realize that there is no one to play the Game at all.

"That there is no me and thus no game. No rising exists as well as not falling, for both exist only in time and space. And time and space exist only in the temple.

"Leave the temple by knowing the You you truly are, the You you have always been and always will be. The You that is always aware of itSelf.

"Never has there been a me and a you, a then and a there. Never has there existed a Game nor will there ever be one.

"For there is only the ever-aware Self that has never been lost and that has never gone looking to get back home.

"This is the path of Knowledge.

"The sword of the intellect must be sharp indeed, cutting away all that is false, and keeping only the True, the Permanent."

******

"I believe I understand," I said, "for I have had such moments of seeing all around me as God, and in being in that timeless essence of the Self, as well.

"However, there seems to be a contradiction in what you were saying about the devotees of that teacher who became bitten by the snake, that they were caught up in delusion and really did not want to see the truth, in relation to the two paths of love and knowledge. On the first path one would see a teacher, as well as everyone, as God, forever perfect, ignoring faults. While on the path of knowledge one would see that there is not two in the first place, that there exists no teacher and disciple, with nothing real of permanent happening in the first place. It is all One."

"Yes there is only God; only the One,"

Yama replied. "The world and all in it is nothing but God. You are nothing but God.

"However, until your awareness is firmly established in That, you must deal with relative truth.

"Even a Master, one fully established in the Absolute, may appear to duck from the slash of a swordsman at his neck. And when the sword misses, it simply misses.

"There arises no interpretation of the fact that someone ducked from the blade. Nothing personal has happened. No more will be thought of it.

"Someone who is not acting out of the love of God, but from the fearful place of separation, one must step out of their way. There is no need for retribution. No need to judge them as guilty of a fault.

"See the fault as but a fault, something that will change in time. If faults abound in the character, bless them in the Name of the One who sees all as God, and move on, just as one will move away from a land that is dangerous for its many faults."

"Thank you, teacher, for reminding me not to take events personally."

"Yes, take nothing personally. So many give their power away by reacting to actions of others and even to their words.

"Please explain giving one's power away to others," I asked.

****

Loud voices erupted from the floor beneath our feet.

"You never do anything right!" yelled a woman's voice.

"I'm so sick of your nagging! You make my life hell!" came the retort of a male.

"I'm out of here!"

"Good riddance!"

The door slammed.

"Come, and I will show you what I mean," Yama said, beckoning for me to follow him out the door.

We quickly ran down three flights of stairs and caught up with whom I supposed was the man who had stormed out. He walked out of the building, angrily shoving the entrance door open and stomped down the steps.

"Look at him closely," Yama said. I relaxed my eyes. Then I saw what looked like fishing line streaming back from the man we followed, back to the apartment building. The lines connected with his hands and feet, head and the base of his spine.

"What are these strings attached to him?" I asked.

"His power, you might say. Those are his power lines."

"To what are they connected?"

"To his wife," Yama said. "He thinks he is moving by his own volition. In truth, however, his emotions and thoughts are tied to his wife and her actions.

"He is like a puppet in her hands. If she acts one way he gets upset; if she acts in another, he becomes happy. He is like a bobbing cork in the ocean of her emotions."

We followed him into a nearby bar. He sat at the bar while we took seats in a booth. The husband ordered a couple of whiskeys and threw them down his throat. The bartender said a few consoling words while the man made a few derogatory remarks about his spouse.

"Keep watching," Yama said as we drank our beers.

Blurred shapes, dark things emerged from the floor. Specters or demons they appeared to be. They swirled around the man, their claws scratching at his head. One of them dove into his next shot of whiskey. The man drank it in. More beings arose from the floor as the man pulled at his hair.

"What is happening," I asked, horrified at what I was seeing.

"You can say that he is drinking his words. You make my life hell, he had told his wife. And so she becomes his maker, and indeed he is now going through hell. What maker is not all powerful?"

"How will he get out of this hell?"

"By cutting the strings. By taking responsibility that everything that happens to him is for a reason and that his reactions are his own choice.

"Yet he is not alone."

We walked outside. Pedestrians walked by and cars drove up and down the street. A normal city scene, except now every person, on foot or in a vehicle, had strings streaming behind and in front of them. Everywhere strings stretched. Just like an immense web. A young woman walked by, a giant smile on her face.

"Yama, why is she attached to strings? She looks happy."

"She is happy. However, her boyfriend made her happy. He is now the maker of her happiness. And soon he will become the maker of her unhappiness."

"Everywhere are there strings," I said, awed by the sight.

"It is like a web spun by a monstrous spider."

"It is," Yama said. "This spider is called Maya. She weaves the web of many gods, of many makers, of objects that make people happy or miserable.

"There exists only one Maker, the Self of All That Is, and until people see that, they will continue to be but prey to Maya."

Chapter XVIII
Becoming the Movement of Life; in the ship's wake; the illusion of time; dreamtime

85

"If you can remember to watch yourself like you would watch a leaf floating down the stream, or hear the words of others as though you were listening to the wind, you would be unmoved by the circumstance, while becoming the Movement itself."

"Please explain how one can become the Movement itself," I asked.

We found ourselves on a luxury liner steaming on the sea. No land could we see standing where we stood on the aft, the motor chugging along.

"Do you see that?" Yama asked pointing at the large wake that spread several hundred yards behind.

"Where is the wake in relationship to us?" he asked.

"Behind us," I said.

"Yes, behind us. Does it affect us?

"No, we are ahead of it."

"Well the wake is nothing but the actions of the past, yours and everyone else, as well as their words. Far behind they go, to be witnessed a little moment in the sea of Eternity before disappearing, merging without a trace."

"But does not our past actions cause our present? What about the teaching that we reap what we sow?" I asked.

"If you believe you are a body and that your body is the doer of events along the timeline of past, present and future, then yes, that model of thinking will have you reaping in the future what was done in the past.

"Do you know who rides with us on this ship?"

I looked around and saw no one.

"Come and let us explore," he beckoned.

We traveled the decks and found no one on this immense liner. After going inside we found all the lounges and cabins the same, bereft of any other passengers. On every wall hung wall-to-wall mirrors.

"There is no one on board," I said, very puzzled at the emptiness. "Yet surely someone must be piloting this ship?"

"No one on board? The whole world rides with us."

"What are you talking about?" I said, forgetting the many previous experiences with my guide; until Yama laughed and I knew something must be coming.

"Look in the mirror. What do you see?"

"Just myself and you," I said, looking at our images stretching into Eternity with the mirror behind us.

"Look again."

When I returned my gaze from Yama to the mirror, I not only saw myself but my parents, my siblings, grandparents, friends, faces that looked familiar, enemies, people dressed in all manners of clothing, both of modern and ancient dress and attire to come, historical figures, both of noble and disreputable character—all stretching in a line without end.

I muttered that I did not understand.

I saw Napoleon, Cleopatra, Hitler, Jesus, Kabir, the Beatles....

"All are notions in your mind. All of these notions, these characters in time, are but froth in the wake of the ship, of life."

"Is there nothing to learn from history, from the actions, whether great or ill, of those who came before—or at least seemed to come before?"

I asked, my mind feeling twisted in knots. I was speaking about a past that does not exist and trying to speak timelessly with a language with a variety of tenses; it was indeed just too mind boggling.

Yama led me back aft and looked at the wake awhile before saying anything.

"Fine, for the sake of argument we will suppose there exists time, that you are born, you will grow older, moving through an infant's body, to a child's, a youth's, a young man's, a middle-aged one, and finally to an elder's. Then I come along and tap your shoulder and off your body goes back to dust.

"Most who walk this world, upon the road of time, believe this reality and do not question this. And for them time's function is to allow enough opportunities to do and acquire all that they want.

"They see the past as the root of the present and the future the fruits. Believing in time history can teach them about what has worked and what has failed.

"Now the problem is that one may look upon any past event, and pending on points of view, view it as successful or failing, and only a fraction of the past can be viewed at anytime; and usually only the past that fits into the model of the present outlook will be seen. For instance, someone who believes they are but a victim in a cruel universe will look back and remember all the moments that reinforce that idea, while eschewing any events that might contradict such a notion.

"The images of the past are constantly shimmering, like a mirage in the desert, because in truth, that is what they are.

"In truth, the past, or the concept of having a past, is one's vain attempt of continuing to dream the dream of time and not wake up into Eternity.

"The Masters, those who rest in the timeless knowing of Eternity, use time only because their students believe in it. They give all sorts of techniques and disciplines to bring a student closer to waking up, to being timeless, by making use of time.

"Just as you are not your body, or your emotions or your thoughts, still they can be used by Spirit to come to the place where you know you are not those.

"So it is with time.

"In time there appears to be unfolding, of cause and effect, sequences after sequences."

"From my perception, dear teacher, I see event leading to event."

"You are dreaming right now. Yet you know it is a dream, so my jumping around from space to space and time to time seems quite extraordinary to you because you have a waking consciousness with its own 'normal' laws of reality of which I seem to bend.

"However, if you were in a dreaming consciousness, where you would behold this dream as being awake, being in the real world, your mind would tie my actions together by creating the illusion of a sequential unfolding of time."

"I don't understand. Have patience and please explain further."

"As a child you created a little book where you placed a dot on each page, placing on each at a different spot. When you flipped the pages quickly, the dot appeared to be moving. But it was just an illusion, a trick of the mind to connect each page.

"In truth, reality is just being the dot in each moment."

"How do I do that? How do I realize being just a dot in the moment, not believing in a past or a future?" I asked. "Are you trying to turn me into a dotard?" I continued, now trying to be funny.

Ignoring my humor Yama said, "When all your experiences with me are written in a book form."

"I will write all this in a book?"

"Yes."

"But isn't that the future? If there is no future—"

"The future is simply another dot in another position," Yama replied.

"And I am aware of all dots in all positions, simultaneously. They are like dots in a larger dot."

There arose that feeling again (again? But there is no again ...) of trying to picture simultaneously little nows within larger nows, within larger nows ... .

"Anyway," Yama continued, "The reader of this book will hear your question about how to just be the dot and will think that I have already answered this question, because he or she reads from beginning to finish, from sequence to sequence.

"However, if the reader just opened it to this dot in the larger dot of this dream, there exist only the question and the answer.

"That is why the Master is infinitely patient, why God is so, because there exist no repeated lessons.

"Watch a child. When a child is happy, say suckling, the child is completely happy. No thought arises saying that this happiness will pass. It is eternally in the Moment.

"Take the child away from that breast when hunger still persists and no hope of the breast ever returning enters. And the child is in eternal torment.

"For some time the child will have no concepts, no tying together of moments.

"Your book will be a book of moments, of questions and answers. Many will find contradiction in my teachings. But contradictions are found in sequences, where the logic of the intellect reigns.

"To go beyond the place of death, of time, to the truth, answers are for only the Moment."

"Fine," I said, "I can see that it is true for a small child. Yet, after all, their scope of needs and awareness is much smaller than an adult's. But for me as an adult, I can see the progression of things; how things got to be where they are.

"For instance, if there is a pile of books on the floor, someone placed them there. They did not appear just out of thin air."

"They didn't?" Yama asked with his mischievous smile. "How do you know they did not?"

"Because I would remember putting them there."

Yama nodded. "We'll see."

And with that he waved his arms.

****

I pulled out my .32 pistol and began firing at the Russian agents. Three of them have trapped me in the large warehouse; their mission; to take me either dead or alive. For too long—ten long years—I have been a thorn in their intelligence operations. As one of the KGB pinned me down with fire, I knew the others were flanking me. I must escape to get word back to the Agency about the terrorist plot. Hell, I've been in worst situations before. Carefully, I took out the pen that was in fact a high explosive. I'll show those ... .

"Wake up!" Yama shouted as he stood over me.

"What are you doing? I want to know if I escaped or not," I mumbled sleepily.

"Oh how we want to sleep and to continue the drama.

"What were you doing?" he asked.

"Dreaming, I guess; although if this is a dream I was dreaming within a dream."

"What do you think the secret agent would have said if I asked him the same question?"

"Probably he would have said that he was fighting Russian agents."

"Do you think he believed that a past led up to that moment in the warehouse, complete with his own complicated history, as well as a probable future?"

"Definitely," I said, "and the future was a bleak one if he could not get word back to the Agency."

"However, was there a past and will there be a future for him?"

"No, it was just a dream."

"But could you tell him—that you that?" Yama asked.

"No. Yet is not a dream different? After all, in waking consciousness one has many dreams throughout their long life. Each night is a new dream, but there is always waking up to the same you with the same job, the same wife, etc."

"Perhaps. Yet if you would have asked that agent if he slept and woke up always the same and whether he had dreams, what do you suppose he would have said?"

I knew Yama got me again. Intuitively I knew the answer.

Yama nodded and smiled. "There is only the Moment. And the mind, like a spider, weaves around it a web of past and future."

****

I closed my eyes and watched my breath, my mind becoming quiet. Like a stone removed from a brook, the waters of peace rushed in. For a while I sat thus, timeless. Then my eyes opened and I saw a pile of books in front of me.

I smiled at Yama. "Very funny. I get your point. Still, I am a schoolteacher and I do like books. Is there no point in reading books of history?"

Yama sighed and said, "Mindless and at peace one moment; now full of questions and restless.

"Enjoy your books, enjoy your history. Just know that they are only dream fragments as well. Appreciate this consciousness that creates all of it."

My mind was ready with a new question when he waved his hand again ... .

Chapter XIX

Getting out of the trap; stopping the endless questions; the chain of desires; working with mistakes

Yama and I appeared on a gravel path that led to an old one-room schoolhouse. We could hear loud moans coming from inside. We went in and the room was full of people, from young to old, sitting at desks. Yet what was unusual, and which was the source of the moans of anguish, was that each of these people had a leg caught in a bear trap.

When they saw me standing there in front of the class they all shouted:

"Teacher you have come."

I quickly went to the nearest one, an old man.

"You poor man, let me help you."

"Thank you," he said, his face lighting up. "Then please tell me who made this trap?"

"And when it was made?" asked a young woman.

"And who put them in here?" asked a boy.

"And why they would do such a thing?" asked a girl.

"And where are they from and what is their town like?" asked another man.

"And do they have wars there?"

"What is their favorite food?"

"Why do many people not eat pork?"

"Are small farms a thing of the past?"

"Stop!" I shouted. "Stop these questions. What are you crazy? Let me get these traps off you."

"Oh no," said the first man and the eldest.

"You are our teacher and must answer our questions first."

"But your questions are endless."

He looked dumbly at me for a moment.

"Of course we have questions. We are here to learn. We want knowledge. We want the truth."

"Yes," said a young woman, "do you suppose these traps are the manufacturers' attempt to exercise control over us?"

"Or could there be a conspiracy between the government and the manufacturer?"

"Perhaps these weren't even humans who created the technology for these traps, but actually aliens from another world."

"Aliens? How do you know there is life out there? That's ridiculous!" shouted another.

A big debate arose about the possibility of life on other planets. I shut the door behind me, Yama standing next to me smiling.

"They are mad," I said, the moans once more issuing from the schoolhouse.

"Of course, they are. Just like you."

"Hey, I am not like them. Those idiots are suffering and they are busy asking inane questions, instead of getting to the source of their pain."

"Exactly."

****

After meditating on my experience in the schoolhouse I saw how my questions, which seem so important at the time, are merely distractions from removing the source of suffering. And who can understand anything when they are in the throes of suffering?

"Why do we make it so hard on ourselves?" I asked.

"Let me show you someone."

We sat amongst a group of disciples around a very holy looking man. The teacher beckoned the man sitting next to me over to him.

"You are nearly established in the truth," said the teacher to the disciple. "Go to the spot where I did my austerities. Live simply; focus your time on going inward. Do not leave until I come for you."

The disciple bowed, taking with him his water pot and a spare loincloth. We followed behind. The man came at last to a spot where a crude hut stood next a river. He bowed to the spot and immediately began meditating.

A town was not too distant and some people came to pay respect to this holy man and to offer food. Each day he would wash one loincloth and wear the other. Yet soon they became threadbare and he had to go into town and beg for a loincloth.

Time passed and soon another loincloth wore out, and another, and each time into town he would go begging. Finally, the townspeople came up with an idea.

"Why don't you take a whole roll of cloth so you don't have to come into town?"

"That is a fine idea," he said.

And so he did. It worked well awhile, giving him more time to meditate. But then he noticed that holes were being formed in the cloth. And with every morning new holes he found.

So one night he kept vigil on the cloth and saw a family of rats gnawing at the fabric. He shooed them away; yet no matter how hard he tried to meditate he kept thinking about rats eating his cloth.

Days went by, his meditations plagued by fear. So he went into town and told the townspeople what was happening.

"Simple. Just get a cat to keep them away."

And so he did.

It worked. The rats were kept away and he could meditate peacefully now. Well, until the cat kept meowing. And his meditations ceased.

Back to the town he went.

"The cat has driven the rats away, yet now he just meows.

"He needs milk," they told him.

They filled up his water pot with milk. And the cat stopped meowing.

However, now he had to go and beg milk every

day and soon the townspeople came up with a new idea.

"You need a cow so you can have milk daily without coming into town."

"That's good idea. It will give me more time to meditate."

Thus he took a cow home with him. It worked. Each day the cat had milk. However, grass was spare on his small plot of land, so shortly he found himself going to town to beg for hay.

After a while the townspeople said, "We will give you some land next to your hut so your cow will have plenty to graze upon."

And this too worked. He did not have to go into town for hay. However, he did have to watch the cow for fear of predators and

95

had to take it to various spots for it to graze. Soon he had no time to meditate.

"You need a wife to help you," the people told him after hearing his plight. "Then she will tend the cow."

A marriage was arranged and he had a sweet wife who managed the cow. And finally he could meditate once more.

Yet the rains came and the wife pleaded to her husband to build a barn for her to tend the cow. So he did. Now the cat and the cow and the two of them slept in the barn. Then on one cold night he and his wife snuggled together. Soon with her womb full she said, "It is not right that a child be raised in a barn. We need a house."

So he found a job as a carpenter, earned some money and built a house. And with the first child there was a need for a sibling. And so there was.

Long did time run by without even the thought of meditation, until one day a knock came at the door. The man opened it and saw, standing in front of him, his master. The master did not recognize his student who was wearing normal attire that his wife long ago had asked him to wear.

"I am looking for a sadhu I sent here ten years ago. Do you know where he might be?"

The man fell at his master's feet.

"Teacher, forgive me. I am he."

The master was amazed. "What happened?"

"I just needed a new loincloth!" came the anguished reply.

****

"How easy to become entangled!" I said, after watching the ten-year story flash by as dreams can do. "I look at my tendencies of being practical, and instead of helping me it seems, it is the opposite. The mind is constantly setting up circumstances to be useful, to be listened to, to be in charge.

"Dear Yama, what happens to a man when he finds himself already so entangled? Surely he cannot just leave his family and go spend all his time meditating. Is there a way out?"

"There is always a way out. Every moment God offers an opportunity for remembering one's true nature that is one with God, utilizing every thought, word and deed, even those that entangle one more in externals.

"As an artist can change a mistake into an unforeseen component of his composition, allowing it to transform into a piece of art beyond the initial idea, so does God work with one's mistakes.

"Unfortunately, few allow mistakes to guide them, and to play with them; instead, most people just fight them."

"Fine," I said, "I understand that one can work with mistakes; but what about that sadhu who is now a husband and a father. How does he disentangle himself?"

"By attitude. He must be a sadhu on the inside and a householder on the outside. He acts in the home while keeping his mind on God, letting the wheel of circumstances turn, and hopefully he will learn from his 'mistakes.'"

"Are there not mistakes that are so serious that they cannot be used creatively? I look at my world and I have seen some rather heinous mistakes.

"In fact, I have been on the other end of some people's actions that seemed to be rather deliberate in inflicting pain on me. It was no mistake that my father threw me out of the home. And what about history? Hitler and Stalin did not just make a mistake when they ordered millions killed."

"Didn't they? God is always trying to bring one's awareness back to the Oneness. God, Spirit, sees mistakes only in those terms. What these two did was to sever their Awareness of the Unity of All That Is. And that was their mistake. Spirit has compassion for everyone and sees that I am tired of this game called life and death.

"So every action is an opportunity God uses to free us."

Chapter XX
The prison of the world; holding the key of forgiveness

98

We stood in front of an immense building that stretched from horizon to horizon. Around it wrapped a wicked looking fence with barbed wire, along with guard towers interspersed, manned with armed guards.

"This looks like an enormous penitentiary," I said.

"It is simply the world as most see it."

We were allowed through the gate as we were dressed in guard uniforms. Inside the building dim light penetrated the endless corridor; the smell rancid, the air filled with curses and screams of mercy.

As far as I could see I saw cells, inhabited by pathetic inmates, naked and starved; while in front of each cell stood or sat a guard, each looking only slightly better than their ward, wearing uniforms threadbare and with faces gaunt with hunger.

In each of their hands the guards held a key.

As we walked by each cell both inmates and guards recognized Yama. The inmates begged him for release while the guards saluted fearfully. "Yes, I am the warden of this stinking place," said Yama in a doleful voice. "And how I long to end this job."

Yama pulled out his sword and with a sorrowful, disgusted mien, he would now and then thrust his sword through the bars and kill an inmate or without warning behead a guard. Immediately one or the other would be replaced.

"Who built it?" I asked, shocked, my stomach turning at the carnage as I now slipped on the bloody floor. "And who keeps you in your position?"

"You. You both built it and keep it operating."

"I?" I stopped, feeling an unexpected rage rising within me. "Don't you dare put this on me. I have never seen this hellhole before, let alone would I have anything to do with constructing such a heinous place of suffering."

With a sternness I had not seen in Yama, he said, "We will see about that."

Fuming, I continued walking with him, silent outwardly, but my thoughts screaming at his accusation. We came to a small square where four corridors led from it in each direction. In the middle of the square I saw a cell covered in shadow; its inhabitant lost in its darkness. A guard sat in front, his back to us.

My heart began beating faster.

"Why have you brought me here?" I said accusingly.

"Behold the inmate."

I slowly moved past the guard without looking at him, compelled despite my resistance, my eyes staring straight ahead. Then out of the shadows he stepped forward. Out of the death camps he looked, a living skeleton. Then I noticed his face, and although so emaciated, I recognized him!

"Father?" I muttered, not believing my eyes. At the sound of my voice he fled back into the shadows.

I turned to the guard to demand the key. Yet as I did so the guard was not there. It was only I sitting there, the key in my hand. I stared at the cell. There was only the cell to be aware of, and my ward. That was my job. Dimly in my awareness I could hear the echoing of footsteps coming down the hall and the sound of the occasional scrape of metal, a scream and a thud.

Coming closer. The Warden.

I stared at my emaciated father, his hands stretching towards me, his eyes pleading.

"Don't look at me like that. Why should you be free? You have abandoned me, disowned me as your son," I snarled at him.

He looked back silently. Then, all of a sudden, his face became fuzzy. I blinked. Looking back at me was no longer my father, but my mother.

"Mother, why are you here? This is no place for you."

Then in rapid succession, the faces of the prisoner changed—my brothers, my sister, my nanny, old childhood friends, foes, lovers, my son, my wife and finally my own face stared back at me.

"Stop this! This is trickery!" I shouted, clutching at the bars. The prisoner, now with my father's face, once more gazed at me.

The prisoner, my father, said to me, "Free me and you free yourself and everyone with you."

The footsteps of the warden echoed closer. Another swish of the blade and another cry and thump. My heart raced.

It could end with a simple slice of a blade—or would it end? Or I could just turn the lock.

Louder and louder the footfalls came. I could feel the warden's breath.

I turned the key. And I took my father's hand. Tears fell from my eyes as my heart swelled.

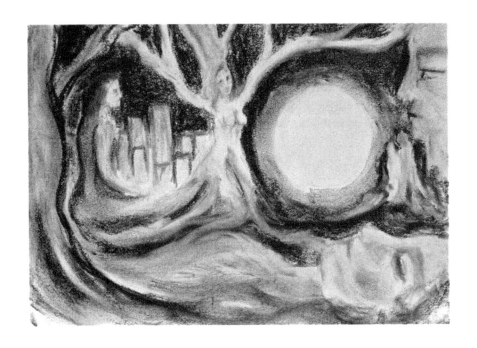

Chapter XXI
The Light behind the scenes; the play of images; becoming the witness; Yama as Dharma

I stood with Yama, the two of us alone in a meadow of lilies. Nowhere could I see the penitentiary. No stench, only the sweetest of fragrances.

"What happened?" I asked, my heart still racing, tears still in my eyes. "Where is the penitentiary?"

"Your father, the penitentiary, have never existed. They were all in your mind—a mind that believed there was an other, something outside of you. This other has myriad faces, masks, if you will, each with a definition you have painted upon them, due to your interpretation of their actions.

"Your father, for example, by his action of disowning you as his son, you have defined him as guilty, and your mother, who accepts you no matter how strange you live, you have defined as kind. By your definitions one was warranted to be imprisoned, the other freed."

"Yet I saw both in the cell."

"Indeed. Any definition is a cell. By imprisoning only one person you imprison everyone, because you are seeing with the eyes of limitations. Whenever you judge anyone by their actions, whether it is by their mistakes or by what are good actions, you have imprisoned them."

"But someone who lives their whole lives doing horrible deeds are surely horrible people," I said.

"Come let me show you something," Yama said.

We walked across the meadow and came to a stone altar. Upon the altar rested a brilliant orb, blazing like a miniature sun. I shaded my eyes, while Yama stared at it unblinkingly. Before the light he bowed.

"What is it?" I asked.

"You might say it is the Self, the eternal, effulgent Being that exists in all beings, all things. Or at least it represents That. In truth one cannot perceive the Self, for it cannot be objectified; it cannot be limited by time and space, as all objects must do to exist.

"One can only know It.

"And one can only know It by being It."

In Yama's hands he suddenly held something that looked like a lampshade. Upon it was one large photograph wrapped around it with images of people and places and creatures.

"What is that?" I asked.

"History. Life." Yama placed the shade around the orb. The light, the orb, illuminated the images of the shade from behind, and as the images became illuminated they began to move across the screen.

I sat down and watched, mesmerized by the scenes moving before me.

****

I watched a little bald-headed man feed people who were little more than bones, and then watched horrified as soldiers on

103

horseback rode down the little man and all the others, their swords flashing red.

I watched a garden rise from spring, reds, yellows, whites, purples, shining forth their splendor, trees blossoming. Then the trees bore fruit while some flowers lost their initial blooms and new flowers began to shine forth. The skies grew darker, the winds blew, leaves changed colors, flowers faded. Soon the ground was white, the trees bare; the garden nowhere to be seen.

I watched a family of quail scurry across a trail, the two parents watching their six little ones. Suddenly out of a bush a bobcat pounced upon them, a little one motionless in the cat's mouth.

I looked at a golden hill, smooth like a woman's breast, the blue sky behind. Then a great shower of dirt and rocks exploded upwards. When the dust settled, the hill was gone, and enormous vehicles moved amongst the stones, searching.

I watched a hundred jets stream down from the sky onto a city with minarets, limbs strewn amongst the rubble, rescuers comforting the wounded, people feeding each other with what they had.

I watched a man paint a castle out of colors with loving care and then go inside and walk over to his wife and backhand her across the mouth.

I watched dirty men in alleys share a whiskey bottle between them, a group of girls at a beach, blooming into womanhood, giggling at a group of young men playing ball.

I watched a little boy and girl playing in a sandbox, a cathedral full of worshipers, and a traffic jam on a knot of a freeway.

I watched a plane full of passengers explode into a skyscraper, a woman giving birth in the shallows at a beach with dolphins swimming around.

Distantly I felt a tap on my left shoulder and faintly heard something. But I forgot the tap and the whispers as I watched a bunch of policeman beating mercilessly some man on the ground.

Then my left ear was violently pulled as I was lifted from my seat. I stared into the face of Yama.

104

"There was a time when a simple tap on the shoulder would get people to take their attention from life. Now I have to resort to pulling ears! My job only gets harder."

"Wow, what horrors you showed me," I said, horrid phantom images floating across my mind's eye.

"And beauty. My, it is so easy for people to remember only the dark things," Yama said, shaking his head disappointingly,

"So what did you learn from my little show?"

"That good and bad exists in the world. You can't have one without the other."

"True. That is if you believe there is good than bad exists as its shadow.

"Well, such observations are at the elementary school of wisdom.

"What about the Orb?" he continued. "What significance does it have?"

"The illumination of the Orb brought the screen to life," I said, hoping to rise up in this school of wisdom.

"That is an accurate observation. Anything else?"

"There is light behind all actions?" I said timidly.

"Good. Continue."

"No action can exist without the illumination of the light, the Self, to make it possible. All actions! No matter what kind, whether beautiful or horrendous, the light allows it to happen, gives it power."

"What happens to the light, the Self, while all this is going on?" Yama asked.

"Nothing! It is untouched. No matter how horrible it is, no actions can touch the Self—the One Self."

"Now we are getting somewhere. Maybe you are reaching high-school level?

"Remember this in all that you see. Remember the Orb. No matter who that person is, what she has done, the one Orb, the one Self, shines within, untouched, never diminished.

"Whether a sinner or a saint."

****

We stayed in silence a long while, watching the show of images. This time I did not see with eyes mesmerized, losing myself in the images as I did before. This time I just watched, witnessed.

Actions one would normally deem bad I witnessed with a stillness of being, seeing past the fleeting forms and remembering the ever-shining Orb behind.

And with what many would deem good I witnessed in the same manner, remembering the Orb.

When I forgot the Orb and got caught in the action, I noticed something surprising.

"Yama, if I forget to behold the light behind the forms, I feel such a disturbance compared to the stillness of remembering the light."

"Yes."

"But it's the same with both the disturbing scenes and the pleasant ones. They both feel the same! How can that be?"

"You are just becoming wiser maybe. It is easy to push away the world when one is in the mud of despair. That is usually when one begins to live a spiritual life, to get out of the suffering.

"But I will not let one stay in suffering because that would be too easy to realize there is no happiness out there, out in the world.

"I will send wonderful situations to such a one; circumstances that they had only dreamed of living, but thought impossible. These delicacies are not so easily pushed away with dispassion"

"As you did with me, offering all those boons if I forsook asking about your mysteries."

"Yes. I was pleasantly surprised."

"But why do you tempt so? Do you not want to end your wearisome job as death?"

"Yes, I desire to end this job; just as a righteous policeman would love to live in a world where he was not needed, or a doctor, or a psychiatrist, a soldier, or an executioner.

"As long as there is one person who identifies with the forms, even if they are just latent in the mind, I must continue the role of executioner.

"And since that is my role, my Dharma, and none is better suited than I to play it, I might as well enjoy it, and do my best.

106

That is why I am the embodiment of Dharma, of duty, because from the beginning of time I have faithfully carried out my role.

"When I see anyone in the world doing their duty with devotion, dedication and diligence, no matter what job, from the most menial to the loftiest, I am pleased.

"Instead of always breathing down their necks as death—although how few humans consciously recognize it as the breath of death, but will, instead, be experienced as insipid fear, anxiety, dread—I will walk alongside, encouraging, protecting and removing obstacles.

"For you see I am king of this world. I reward as Dharma and I punish as death."

****

"Yama, truly you are king of this world, you who hold every mortal's breath, please tell me how one knows when one is standing upon the path of Dharma and not upon the path of death. And please explain that surely there are those who firmly stand upon the Dharmic Path, yet even they are cut down."

"These are worthy questions. I will explain.

The one who stands upon the royal Path of Dharma has no thought he stands upon the path. This one no longer stands, nor walks, nor even runs upon the path, but is the Path. Following Dharma there is no thought for oneself. There is nothing to gain, nothing to lose.

"The one of Dharma is only aware of the Orb, the Self, God, or the Master. They are all the same.

"Such a one has his thoughts only upon the Highest. If the impulse from the Highest is to do a menial job it is done; to write, chant, meditate, it is done. If it is to teach peace and be crucified, it is done.

"There is only the Doing.

"And in terms of I as death coming to such a one, where is the one for me to snatch? They are one with God and how can I touch God?"

"But I know of masters who died of cancer, diabetes, being shot. What about them?" I asked.

107

"Does a cobra die when it sheds its skin? Does a peacock perish when it molts its beautiful feathers? Does the maple become no more when all its leaves fall to the ground?

"Such a one can have his body torn to shreds by lions if that is what is needed by Dharma. But it matters not and affects not the one.

"Remember the shade around the Orb. Whatever happens upon the shade, the action, cannot in one whit touch the Orb. One who thinks of the Orb, becomes the Orb, and can no longer be affected.

"Thus they are free from my touch as death."

"I understand that to be one with God, one becomes free of death and that the Master's body is but a silhouette, his real body being the Eternal Light. Thus when others see the Master nailed, or poisoned or eaten by lions, they are only seeing but a shadow."

"Good," said Yama, smiling.

"Yet," I continued, "what about those like me who do not always think of the highest, who have selfish tendencies, who identify with the body and its actions, can one still follow the path of Dharma?"

"Yes."

"Well, how does one know then? One can hear all sorts of things in one's mind telling one to do this or that, like leaving one's family to preach the word of God or live in a cave, or for that matter, place all of one's earnings on a lottery ticket.

"How does one know that it is not the mind playing tricks to keep that ego alive?"

"Before I explain, remember that everyone is an unique expression of God. And everyone must follow their own particular expression of Divinity and not someone else's.

"Yet many forms have been set up: religions, scriptures, philosophies, teachings. These are the corrals for when the foal is young and foolish. Without the corral the foal would run unmindful about, doing just what it would like, while the lions, and jackals, and poisonous plants, waited outside.

"Just as an artist must learn and master a particular tradition before breaking away and expressing in a unique way, so too does the seeker must follow his tradition, its roles and mores, before leaving its boundaries.

"Following these roles in the tradition is Dharma. The wife doing the wife's role, the husband the husband's, the police officer his, etc. until it is Dharma to grow beyond it."

"Still, how does one know it is time to grow beyond, that one is not jumping the fence before the gate is opened?" I asked.

"Who says the gate will be opened for you? Following Dharma is not easy. When you jump the fence you can rest assured that temptations will try to catch you.

"And for you not to run away from the corral and retreat back into its safety would be un-dharmic."

I let loose a big sigh of exasperation.

"It is nearly impossible to tell what one should do to walk the Path of Dharma by using the reasoning of the mind," Yama said.

"The more one sits in the silence of meditation, repeats the holy names and mantras, prays, helping others with the knowledge that the other is but one's Self, harming none, speaking the truth, staying focused in one's activity, and practicing kindness of speech, thought and deeds, then one knows more and more what to do.

"And if you do not know what to do, stay where you are, practicing all of the above. You can be certain that Dharma is asking for you to make change when a calmness, a quiet, and certainty is involved, despite any opposition from others or circumstances.

"A powerful humility is experienced.

"If there is a frantic quality to it, a hastiness, a boastfulness, the mind agitated, a grandiosity associated with the change, no doubt death is breathing upon your neck."

****

"I think I understand," I said. "One should do one's duty and do it well, focusing on one's inner connection with God, and developing virtues outwardly.

"Living in that manner it seems a lot easier to tell where I stand, but will such a criteria give me an idea about whether or not someone else is walking the path, unless perhaps their actions may not be virtuous."

Yama smiled and shook his head.

"Oh, I forgot to mention that to walk upon the Path of Dharma and not the path of death, you must not be concerned about where others may be treading."

"What about following a leader, a teacher, a priest? Didn't you say that one should observe others objectively and not be blinded by what you want to see?"

"Observing someone's character is discrimination. Discrimination about whether that person's company can help you walk upon your path of evolution, upon the path of your Dharma.

"You do not have the ability to judge where the person is walking. Only I and God know that."

Yama's eyes blazed with emphasis, making me cringe.

"Besides," he continued in a stern, severe, voice, "you cannot judge the inner by the outer."

Chapter XXII
Learning to hiss

We stood outside an African village as two old holy men. There was a great commotion and wailing. I followed Yama as we pushed through a crowd of people who were trying to glimpse what was transpiring in a hut. Upon a bed lay a young girl whose leg was swelling and discoloring horribly. Her eyes rolled up in her head and she gasped for breath. Family members lamented.

Yama pushed his way through and placed his hand on her leg and heart. Immediately she calmed down.

"Look, the leg!" cried the father.

The leg began to return to normal.

"Let her rest. She still has a long life ahead," Yama said in a reassuring tone.

After an abundance of crying in gratitude the family informed us that a cobra that lived near the river had bitten the girl. We soon departed after feasting and made our way to the river.

"It should be around here," Yama said. "There it is."

An enormous cobra lay upon the trail in front of us, coiled, hood raised. Yama, unflinchingly, strode up to the serpent. As Yama neared, recognition came to the creature.

"Yama," it hissed, "have you come for me?"

"Perhaps. What you did was not right action. The girl meant you no harm. It was out of spite that you struck her."

"You speak truly, O King of Death. Command me and I shall do it."

"Very well. You shall bite none as your penance."

"I will drink only water and milk for the rest of my days," hissed the cobra before bowing and slipping into the brush.

"What will happen to the cobra?" I asked.

"We shall see. In the meantime let us close our eyes to this dream. Letting all images, all thoughts, slip past our awareness and rest only in That, in that timelessness, unrestricted by any space."

Like a snake shedding its skin I slipped out of body consciousness, mental consciousness, the ego or individual consciousness that believes I am separate from the Great Wholiness and into That I melted.

Peace.
Bliss.
Eternal Awareness.

****

Then I heard a sound, a whisper. I had an ear. The words fell into this ear. Then more Awareness. I had a whole body. And when I opened my eyes I saw Yama, still an African holy man, beckoning to me.

"Time to check on our friend, the cobra."

"We just left it," I said.

Yama laughed and said, "Do you always trust in your sense of time? It is too capricious for that."

We came to another part of the river. A small group of children were jumping up and down, yelling, laughing and throwing sticks and stones at something ahead of them.

"What are you children doing?" I said to some of them.

"We are making sport of the snake that is more like a worm," replied a boy.

As we made our way through this little throng we saw the cobra, its body looked emaciated, covered with scabs and bleeding cuts. Stones and sticks flew at it as it timidly hid its head in its coil.

"Go!" shouted Yama to the children as he raised a stick.

The children all fled. After they had disappeared, just as we were moving closer to the snake, two young men strode up.

"Here it is, the worm-snake," said one of them. "Watch this."

He grabbed the tail of the cobra to the horror of his companion.

"Careful, it will strike you!" the other cried.

"I told you, he is no serpent. It is a worm."

Around and around he spun the cobra, holding it with both hands, spinning like a macabre wheel. The other man started to laugh at the sight of his friend twirling the beast. Then the man let go of the tail and off flew the cobra into a tree, where it slid down stunned.

"You are brave to do that," said his friend to the antagonist. "The women will love the story of your feat."

"You are right. Let us go and tell the tale."

And off they went.

We walked over to the barely moving snake.

"Yama," it barely hissed, "I have harmed none for seven moons now."

"Seven moons?" I said.

Yama gave me his all-knowing look. He kneeled down and put his hand on the twisted body.

"Silly fool of a snake. I asked you not to bite any creature. I did not ask you to become a weakling, a worm."

"I do not understand, Great Yama," replied the cobra.

"By becoming a weakling you have caused as much harm as your biting out of spite."

I looked aghast at Yama.

"Forgive me," said the snake. "Please, Master of all creatures, tell me how."

"By becoming timid, and not being firm, you become a depression on the earth for the stagnant waters of hatred and violence and rage and cowardice to find a place to find a home. Such timidity encourages others to wrong action."

"But what should I have done?"

"Hissed."

"Hissed?" I asked.

"Yes. You must hiss. But to hiss without any thought for your protection, without any anger, or any thought of biting.

"Just as I yelled at the children to be gone, not for my personal gain and without any anger towards them, I did so to keep them from doing wrong action—from harming themselves by harming you.

"Hiss, my child. Rise royally as the king of all serpents that you are, spread that hood in mock anger, and laugh at life's joke as they run away, those that would do harm."

The cobra kissed Yama's feet before it slithered slowly away.

As we continued walking, I said to my constant companion, "I would love to see the faces of those who will try to harm our cobra."

Just then, three young children came screaming down the path towards us, tears lining their faces.

"Run! Run! A cobra tried to kill us!"

We laughed heartily as they sped on by crying for their parents.

Chapter XXIII
The biggest fool; preparing for the inevitable journey

Yama and I strolled in a marketplace what looked to be medieval European: Farmers had their foods displayed, craftsmen their crafts, jewelers their jewels. Over fire pits meat turned on spits. Women in bodices jiggled and men at arms patrolled the streets.

"Yama, I truly know what my happiness is. I know it. Yet the world has many enticements to confuse my mind," I said after a lovely lady blushed at my approach.

"I am such a fool."

"All are fools. But there are fools chasing after things in the world, those things that will bring them happiness they believe. As well as fools in love with God; who want only God.

"And then there are those in between, moving from one end to the other, vacillating between the two."

"Who is the biggest fool?" I asked, hoping he would not point at me.

"He's just around the corner," said Yama, smiling. "I had a funny feeling you would ask."

All of a sudden Yama was wearing a jester's outfit, complete with bells dangling on his feet and hat. He shook his head and kicked his feet together making a little jingle.

"I like these bells," he said, "maybe I should use them all the time so people would know I was coming and begin living truly."

"You're the biggest fool?" I said.

Then I heard the ringing from shoes and noticed that I too was dressed the fool.

"Am I the biggest?"

"Well, not quite, there is at least a bigger one. Let us go visit the king."

The guards of the castle let us in as the king was always ready for entertainment. We bowed to the king who sat upon his golden throne with a group of men looking regal in their liveries.

"Jesters, you who live the lives of fools, tell me who is the greatest fool," asked the king.

"Your Majesty," replied Yama, "I will gladly give you the answer. But first tell me who are these men standing beside you?"

"These are my ministers."

"And what function do they serve?"

"They are my eyes and ears. They go out into my kingdom and tell me all I need to know. And when I travel abroad I send them forth that I may know what awaits me and prepare accordingly.

"That is why I am deemed the wisest of kings. For a man who blindly moves into the future without preparing surely is a fool.

"So tell me, jester, who is the biggest fool that you have come across?"

"You are indeed correct, Your Majesty, a wise man uses all his resources at hand to prepare for a journey, so he can benefit fully.

"That is why, dear king, you who prepare for all your journeys in the world, yet who has neglected to contemplate about the one inevitable journey, surely is the greatest fool."

The king arose red faced.

"What journey do you speak of, FOOL?"

"Death. The journey that all men must take."

And with his dramatic flair, he turned into that horrifying medieval image of a robed skeleton holding a scythe. I could only laugh as I saw the king and all his ministers flee.

What a game, I said to myself as I shook my rattle.

****

With his grinning skull's head, Yama stood impassively for a while, looking upon where all had fled. When he turned back into the fool I felt a little uncertain.

"What is wrong?" he said to me.

"Well, while everybody fled as fast as they could from the sight of you, I just stood here amused, shaking my rattle."

"Yes?"

"Is it not strange? Should I not be terrified in death's presence?"

"You and everyone else are always in my presence. I do not want you to be terrified of me. I want you to love me.

"Then why the terrible guise, you might ask? Do you think I chose such an appearance? I appeared as the king viewed death. He views it fearfully, for he has not prepared to meet me.

"He has pushed me aside, not wanting to look at who I really am. Instead, I have become a little nagging memory in the dark recess of his mind, which keeps growing until I will come for him at last—the embodiment of his fear.

"If he faced me fearlessly, he would accept me as his constant companion. And if he accepted me as such he would grow to love me. And acceptance and love always creates kindness, and thus he would see me in a kinder form."

"Was he really the biggest fool?" I asked.

"Not really. No more than most kings and people who have all that the world can offer them. It is so difficult for such people to see that they can no more control and hold onto their lives as they can hold their breath."

Chapter XXIV
*Pursuing goals; the blood of chasing desires; where attainment
lies; intercourse*

118

"Is it just a fool's dream then to pursue the things of the world? Surely poverty is no better," I said.

"Where are we right now?" he asked me.

"In the king's palace," I replied uncertainly.

"Are we really?"

"Actually," I said, "I guess I am dreaming."

"Yes. You ARE dreaming. And that should be enough of an answer about whether to pursue things of the world if it is only dream stuff.

"However, I can see you still need some more examples. Come with me."

****

We stood somewhere in total darkness. My feet were bare and I could feel dry grass under me. The air felt warm and still.

"Yama,"

I whispered loudly, "where are you?"

"I am right next to you."

"Where are we?"

"You might say we are on a safari."

"What are we after?"

"The world. Follow me."

"I can't see you."

"Just follow the noise."

"What noise?"

Just then loud trumpeting erupted ahead of us.

"Elephants?"

I asked.

"Yes, the world's pursuits. All kings have an elephant. Touch one and it will be yours."

So I began to stumble after the trumpeting, gingerly, feeling my way with my feet. Suddenly, I felt a warm squishiness between my toes.

"Yuck!" I said, lifting my foot up out of this unseen ooze.

"Just keep going. Remember the elephant!"

I took a few more steps and again a squish.

"Keep going!"

And soon I felt again the warmth between my toes. I reached down and stuck my finger in the sludge, bringing it to my nose.

"This smells like shit!" I cried.

Yama erupted in laughter.

"Such is the price of catching elephants!"

"Forget it! I am not walking through this,' I said in complete disgust.

Making sure I found a clear spot I flopped down. I heard Yama sitting down next to me, laughing in bursts. At first I kept thinking about the crap between my toes, and what a rotten trick Yama pulled on me. Anger began to rise the more I thought about it and the more he laughed.

"Relax," Yama said soothingly. "Watch your breath."

Although still feeling angry I began watching my breath. Gradually thoughts about what had happened vanished and contentment came with the quiet.

I sat. Silence. Subtle breath.

Then came awareness of large footfalls nearing. Then stopping. I felt what seemed to be a large serpent wiggle upon my head.

I opened my eyes in the light of early dawn, and stared at an enormous elephant. The elephant trumpeted and lowered its massive body onto its knees.

"Behold," I heard Yama say, "The world has come to you. Mount, O king."

We mounted on the great beast and began walking across the plains, watching the movement of the plain's creatures.

"Why did the elephant come to me?" I asked after a while.

"You became wise. And all that is needed come to the wise."

"How did I become wise? I just got disgusted with stepping in the shit. It wasn't worth it."

"Let me ask you: How many in the world would have given up stepping in the piles if they could have whatever they desired?"

"Putting it that way," I said, "probably not many."

"There is nothing wrong with what the world offers; after all, there is only One and all exists within the One and the One exists in all. It is the pursuit of anything or anyone that creates the feeling of separation. And no greater pain exists than separation.

"The wise live at peace in their Being and utilizes what comes to them to move in the world.

"They chase nothing.

"They want nothing."

****

"I know what you are saying is true, my teacher," I said, my heart feeling suddenly melancholic. "I know it from my experiences. Yet there is an emptiness I feel."

"What emptiness?"

"I long for my wife."

"Your wife? You are married?"

"Yes, for seven years."

"Are you? How do you know?"

"I remember the day we married."

"Oh yes, those reliable images of the mind," he said.

My mind began to waver with a sudden uncertainty. It would not be the first time Yama has shown that the mind is most artful in deceptions and creating fantasies.

"I am married, right? When I wake up I will be lying in bed next to my wife."

"As you say," Yama said with one of those grins. "You were speaking about longing for her."

"I want her to love me. She is in love with another man, and for years has lost any desire for physical intimacy with me," I said, surprised that tears streamed down my cheeks.

"All other pursuits are not worth pursuing through the manure. But this is love. It seems different somehow."

"Is it? Perhaps yes. Perhaps no."

****

We stood in some funeral grounds. Smoke filled the air and my nostrils with the smell of burning flesh. Crackling sounds of fires consuming wood, skin and bones, and skulls popping open resounded in my ears, as well as mantras droning from presiding priests and yogis performing austerities, with waves of wailing

121

from onlookers. Some of the pyres lay quiet with a few wisps of smoke, a few bones strewn about.

Several stray dogs sniffed about the ashes.

"Look at that one," Yama said, pointing at a scrawny mutt. "Here comes your family counselor."

The dog hesitantly approached us, its tail between its legs. Yama picked up what looked a remnant of a leg bone and tossed it to the dog.

The dog sniffed it at first and then began to chew. It cracked the bone open, no doubt hoping for some marrow. Yet nothing but dryness did it find.

Just as it dropped the bone to the ground in disgust, several drops of blood from its gums dripped onto the bone.

The dog licked the blood. And began to chew some more.

Now the more the dog chewed the more its gums were cut and the more blood flowed.

"How pathetic," I said, watching this poor creature misguidedly inflict pain on itself. "It thinks it has found a juicy bone; instead of realizing it is its own blood it is after."

"It is pathetic indeed."

"So why do you call this dog my family counselor?"

"Well, are you not doing the same with your wife? Did you not find her juicy in the beginning and now you are lamenting because you cannot taste any more juice?"

I stammered incoherently, not liking the feeling in my gut.

"Do you think she or anyone can give you juiciness? Anyone you want something from becomes nothing more than a dried bone."

"Why?"

"Because life is about giving, about serving, and about receiving what is given to you. Grabbing anything or anyone is like a dog grabbing for a bone."

"But that sweetness I tasted in the beginning as we made love, becoming one spiritually as well as physically, that is what I want again."

"Don't you see? What you tasted was but your Self, after chasing after the dream of having the perfect mate—your soul mate. The desire for such a one is nothing but a dry bone.

"And you thought you found the ideal mate who would provide all that you wanted from a partner, you began to chew, and chew and chew, never realizing that the bliss you experienced was but a taste of That which is inside of you.

"And while you get tastes of joy, the pain from the chewing grows.

"So you chew more hoping the taste will make you forget the pain."

His words deflated me of all strength and I fell on the ground onto my knees amongst the ashes.

"But it seems natural that a husband and a wife express their love and caring by making love. Isn't making love another form of communication just as speaking is?"

"The only real communication is communion, and communion only happens in the Silence of the One Self.

"However, as long as there is the notion of two, of husband and wife, I can use the desire to speak and the desire to physically unite to move two closer to knowing they are but One.

"Yet I can do that only to a certain extent. There comes a time when both oral and physical intercourse must be transcended."

"How does one know when it is time to go beyond them? How does one know if one is not simply avoiding such communication because of inadequacies?"

"Know that if there is a repulsion, a disgust, at attempting either form, there is most likely still work to do in that area.

"That is why monks and nuns usually must return on the wheel and experience the mastering of finding peace, unconditional happiness, in the chaos of the market place where people rub against one another."

****

I reflected awhile on Yama's words, sitting in the ashes, on my relationship with my wife.

"Will an enlightened couple end up abstaining from sex and be silent, letting words drop as meaningless?" I asked.

"Remember the king who was surrounded by wives and riches and then saw it all fade away? Every night he had pleased a wife and he talked for their pleasure. However, he had no need to. He gained nothing by coupling with them, nor in conversing. Nor did he lose anything either.

"In truth, the king had transcended sex and words for expressing love, as well as transcending celibacy and silence."

"In other words," I said, "I would not be able to tell by the actions of a couple whether they had reached true communion."

"Good. You are learning that actions can tell little about one's state of awareness."

"Still, it would seem that as one did not need anything to be happy, one becomes ever simpler, and so sexual and oral intercourse would naturally fall away," I continued.

"So it would seem," Yama said smiling.

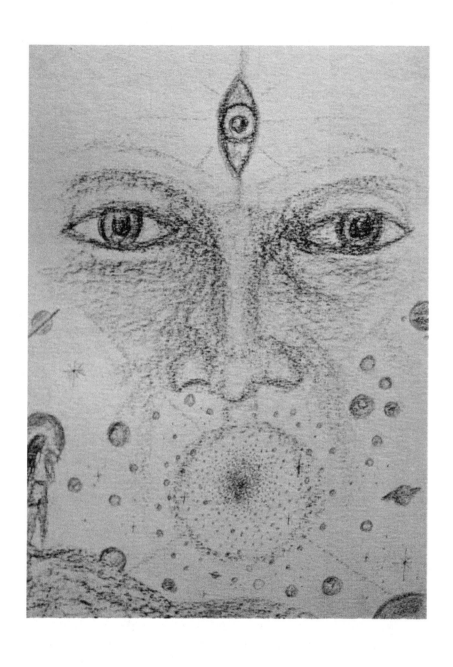

Chapter XXV
Suppression; creative expression; being played by the Player; the Song; disharmony; this age; the dream of suffering

125

How sweet it would be, I thought, to be free of such desires. Ahh, to be a monk. Yes, to be a monk, living simply, no complications of relationship and tripping over words.

It was as though my thoughts propelled me. I sat facing a wall, my legs under the cushion I sat upon. I wore a dark gray robe, the reverberations of a gong fading away. I looked around and saw every wall of the simple hall had bald-headed people dressed as I, arising from their cushions and silently walking out. I followed, touching my head and feeling smooth skin.

As I walked through the well-groomed grounds, I realized I must be in a Zen monastery. Smiling at that thought, the cool breeze of the morning caressed my naked scalp. I breathed in the grayness of the morning before the sun showed itself over the canyon walls, a river gurgling nearby.

This is the life for me, I thought and all remembrance of Yama vanished. I was a Zen monk, and had been for years. Every day after zazen I would go to my garden and water, weed, rake, crumple any clay clods into dust, add compost; harvest, tend, seed or plant. I knew every plant intimately in the garden. I knew how the shadows of the sycamore moved amongst the vegetable rows, throughout the day and year.

Like my plants thriving under my care, I thrived in the silence of the monastery. My relations to my brothers and sisters amounted to bowing as we passed each other upon the gravel path. The two daily meals consisted of silence and gestures for the soy sauce.

As with the stream, time just flowed from one day to the next.

Then one day I awoke before the ringing of the bell for the call to rise, as was my habit. Yet when I heard the bell I did not feel like getting up, I felt like staying in bed and reading. I remembered having such thoughts, thoughts of old-world patterns, which were quickly cast aside by simply following in the rhythm of the framework of the day. This time, however, the thought to read was supported by the will to do so

.In my simple room, bereft of things, save a mattress, a river rock and a Buddha on a shelf and a little bowl of sand for incense, there was a closet where my garden clothes hung.

And a chest.

In the chest, my old books waited; their titles forgotten. How long has it been since light fell into the box?

I opened it. Paints and papers drew my attention first. Then the wooden flute. Pen and paper. Books upon books. Each was like the strata in the surrounding cliffs, layers of desires I had left unfulfilled.

I picked up the flute, the cedar wood smooth to my caress. The wooden key carved into the shape of an eagle in the Native American tradition, leather strips dangling. I placed my fingers on the six round holes and saw the memory of me as an adolescent sitting on the toilet behind closed doors, exploring new-found abilities of my body. What if I'm discovered?

I played the lowest note. It did not break the silence of the morning. It plunged into it. And out of the silence arose another note, bringing the silence with its voice, as the doves and quails and even the jays do. They can tarnish the silence no more than the crashing waves disrupt the depths of the ocean.

Invisible hair stood upon my neck in the resonance, the communion, I felt I was.

And my fingers danced upon the holes as the Breath was blown into my body, my Soul, passing through into the cedar tube and out into the silence of the morning.

The Breath. It's Voice. The Silence.

The Three danced and became One. The flute and I no different; both of us played by an invisible Hand.

Then a knock and the crash of silence. The door opened and the abbot looked at me with saddened eyes.

I bowed. I placed the flute into the chest and closed its lid, and carried the chest in my arms as though I held a fallen comrade, and made my way out the door, onto the path to the monastery's gate.

As I walked through the gate I heard the sounds of a flute leading me onward.

****

Yama sat on top of a boulder, the same flute I had played he played. The arid landscape was as red as his skin. I lay in the scant

127

shade of a sagebrush. My skin too was that of the land, and I wore only a loincloth as Yama did.

Yama stopped playing and asked if I had a nice nap.

Again another dream within a dream. How many dreams? How many layers is this dream? And which layer am I in now? I thought as I sat up.

"Do you remember your dream?"

"I do."

"And do you still want to be a monk?"

"No, although I enjoyed my time as one. The simplicity. Yet it did not feel right anymore."

"Why?"

"Because something else was being called to be expressed through me," I said.

"Just as you felt the Breath playing through you?"

"Yes. It was as though all those years of silence, and living such a simplistic life, I was like a flute being carved, smoothed. And then the time came for me to be played.

"Is it like that for all monks and those living a quiet, removed life from the world?" I asked. "Are they being fashioned, prepared to go back?"

"Every soul has a different path. One may end one's life as a monk or as anything else. There is no telling how one should end up. For you, you still needed to express desires given to you, as was being a monk a desire."

"Yet do not many religious traditions espouse the monastic life as the final stage before liberation, after giving up all other desires?" I asked.

"Behold this flute and what the Ancestors knew about the meaning of the flute."

****

Yama breathed in, taking a mighty breath. Time stopped. The world began to reel, shimmer, and become as smoke, like breathing amidst the fog. My body vaporized and all things began to flow towards Yama. My Awareness, along with everything else, rushed into his mouth. Into the Silence of his Being.

128

And there was only That.
No thing.
No thoughts.
Free of all form.
Not blackness.
Not light.
Being.
Essence.
I was.
Was not.
Then a thrill. A flutter.
An immense joy burst forth.
Arising I was, I AM.

That in which I arose loved me as it Self; and I loved That as my Self. And in that joy I uttered my joy, my Self. Out into That, yet not leaving That, I emerged.

And all around me and within me other sounds of joy resounded: Within the Silence, within the space of Being. Each note penetrating that living space, plunging into it, wrapping itself in that Bliss, like a caterpillar enshrouding itself in its silk, gathering, forming, shaping themselves into worlds.

Growing.
Becoming.
Fulfilling the Breath of the Player.
Until the Pause, and the in-breath and all the forms dissolved.
Back into the Silence.

****

I opened my eyes and found myself sitting in the shade of the sagebrush and fell at Yama's feet as he lifted the flute to the sky in homage.

"Do not worship my feet. I only played a song.

"All beings are being played by the Player. The Player's Breath animates all forms, gross and subtle.

"As with you, your consciousness arises out of the deep silence, you move about, feel, think, experience and then the end of the day comes, the energy of consciousness withdraws, the body first, then the feelings and thoughts of dreams withdraw and back falls consciousness into the silent depths.

"Every breath you take the Player plays you. All things breathe. Even the stones themselves. Worlds. All are being breathed into becoming.

"All things, all forms, are notes in the Great Song of Becoming.

"All traditions, all lifestyles, all beliefs are notes of that Song.

"And this Song of Becoming has no end."

"Yet, when the Player inhales then does not all come to an end?" I asked.

"As a flute player takes in a breath to continue to play the song, so does the Player. However, in this Great Song of Becoming every form plays a song, from the smallest to the great gods. Songs lasting a microsecond to songs universal.

"Songs within songs within songs. Yet all the One Song."

****

Yama closed his eyes, cocking his head as if to listen. Smiling.

I closed my eyes and listened as well. Past the swirling questions and revelations, into the Silence, into the Hum, the OM, the One Chord behind all chords. Around and within.

After a long while we opened our eyes.

"Yama, everywhere this OM pervades. Why do so few hear it?"

Yama stood up and looked over the vast expanse of desert, buttes like faces watching over the land.

"Here, in the living silence of the land, many can hear it. Nature resounds with the Great Song. That is why the people who live with the land, who work with the land and move with its rhythm, have a love for it because they hear the Song. And when the Song is all-important the people thrive; the land thrives.

"Yet when the people listen not to the Song but listen to selfish thoughts, thoughts of taking more than one needs, thoughts that they are simply a body and must do whatever it takes to survive and thoughts of increasing one's pleasure, then the Song recedes to the background and then this is what you have."

****

Over the vast expanse of desert, instead of majestic buttes, tall buildings arose; the red rock, the rich blood of the earth, turned gray like a corpse with cement; the white puffy clouds turning black, spewing out of factory stacks, automobiles racing to and fro like frantic beasts in hunt of prey.

"This is living life in discord, no longer hearing the Chord of Being. Here lies suffering en masse."

My stomach turned at the sudden death of the land. Still I looked for hope.

"Yama, you who prowl such streets, is this not as well, however ugly, still not part of the Song of Becoming?"

"Good. You are learning. Yes, even this is but a note, an off-note, in the Great Song. And the Player is a masterful musician and works this off-note, this dissonance, beautifully into the Song."

"Is there a finale to this Song? Human songs have ends," I said.

"Every song ended has been the beginning of another, whether with one person's life or for humanity as a whole. No song is original. It follows but another. A round of creation, or that Big Cymbal Clash that scientists say is the start of the universe, is but a song after and before another, as well as just a note within a greater song between two other songs."

My mind feebly tried to grasp what Yama said, trying to find an end and a beginning to the Song."

"You mean to tell me that even the Creator is not original?" I said, half-seriously, half-jokingly.

"Exactly," Yama said smiling. "Remember that if anyone tells you your work is not original. You are in good company!"

I laughed.

"However, back to your questions. No, there is no end, no beginning to the Song. And, yes, there is an end to all of this," Yama said pointing to the city below.

"Remember this too will not last. Like a farmer tending his fields, I will cut such weeds down."

****

"Yama, you say this weed of a civilization you will cut down, like a surgeon cutting away a cancerous growth."

"Yes."

"Will there arise a beautiful flower of a civilization in its place?"

"Of course. The Wheel turns forever. There will come a time, and soon, when more and more souls will awaken to love, and who will then act with harmony with the world around.

"Where love reigns, beauty and truth will soon follow."

"Will you be working as death then? If everyone is coming from truth and love, which will be in accord with you as Dharma, death should end, yes?"

"What you say has merit," replied Yama. "In this New World I will not be stalking behind everyone and then unexpectedly slip over the noose.

"Instead, I will walk alongside each one, like a gentleman, ready to open the door for any who want to leave the earth and go to another world, another realm, to do as love dictates."

"Heaven on earth," I said. "Then what? If the only reason is to know one's Self, and the Self is love, is not the game over?"

"Remember the temple and all its many levels. Remember the third level, heaven? And how much farther one still had to travel to reach the top, to reach full consciousness?"

"Yes, and I remember the serpents as well!"

"When heaven and earth join the adventure just continues. Many will go higher and many will get bitten and be taken back down."

"Why?" I asked. "It seems once one finds love again one would be impervious to the serpents."

"Remember the three robbers? There was Tamas the Black; Rajas the Red; and Sattwa the White. These are the qualities of the mind, whether the mind of the individual or the Universal Mind. And in truth there is but One Mind.

"If only Sattwa the pure existed in the mind there would be no Mind, because Sattwa reflects the truth that is timeless. And because all would be timeless, no universe would exist because the universe is the expression of the Mind in time.

"Everything would stop. Desire would cease to be and desire is needed to keep the Game happening. You need to want to play to have a game.

"Thus no matter how pure any condition is, the seeds of Tamas to make things dense and obscure, to veil the Mind in ignorance, will exist; as well as the seeds of Rajas to stir things up."

"Well, what's the point?" I said. "It seems that when heaven on earth occurs humanity will have finally won, winning against all odds, with all our wars and stupidity. The Game should end and a big party should take place."

Yama shook his head and laughed.

"There is no point. In fact, there are no points at all. No points and therefore no winning and losing.

"It is nothing more than playing for the love of playing; expressing, or pressing outward, for the joy of expressing."

****

"All right, I can feel what you say. Still, suffering will have finally ended."

"Suffering?" Yama looked intently at me. "What about your stomach right now?

"My belly began to grumble uncontrollably. Thoughts came into my head that I had not eaten for over a week.

"I'm starving," I said pathetically, the pain becoming more acute with the awareness.

"What do you mean you are starving? Do you not remember that you are only dreaming? You went to bed with a full stomach."

Yama might as well have spoken in another tribal language; for all I could understand was getting some food to assuage my suffering. I was ready to run off with shaky legs in search of food before Yama handed me some strip of dried deer meat. After I had eaten enough to stave off the hunger pains then I was ready to listen once more.

"Now do you remember that you dream?"

133

I nodded.

"Were you truly starving, suffering?"

"No."

"Did I truly feed you?"

"Well, not truly."

"The truth can be said about the Game. The Game is but God's Playing. Things appear to suffer and things appear to help the suffering.

"God does not suffer.

"And you are God.

"You do not suffer.

"You do not help.

"You are simply playing a game in a bubble in the ocean of Eternity.

"Stop thinking about endings," Yama concluded in a staccato manner to emphasize his point.

Chapter XXVI
Attraction; relationship as a means; acting as if dying;
fearlessness

135

"Fine, all is a game. All the world is a great play," I said. "Then please tell me about one of the most complicated play in the Play, the play of relationship."

"If you insist."

We sat in an Italian cafe, in modern garb. This time, however, Yama appeared as an attractive olive-skinned woman, with amazing dark seductive eyes. Although I knew Yama sat before me I could feel my heart race and could feel the warmth in my groin as she crossed her long legs.

"What is wrong?" Yama asked in a coyish manner. "Your nostrils seem to be flaring a bit."

I blushed despite myself.

"Shall we go for a walk?" she said in the same manner, knowing full well that I could not stand without losing any sense of dignity I might have left.

"Why does your attraction to this form embarrass you? It is part of the Game that you want to mate. It keeps the Game going, does it not?"

I just muttered incoherently, no doubt turning redder.

"For whatever reason, perhaps these eyes remind you of your mother's, or these breasts look like those in a men's magazine you fantasized about as a boy, or these legs in a commercial you've seen many times. One can never know why we have attraction to each other, although we may think we do.

"You could have me. But just as with everyone you get the whole package of habits, and faults, pettiness and hidden desires. Don't forget that, no matter how pleasing the package.

"All such things you will have to deal with at some point after you have enjoyed this body."

"But what if I just want to for one time, and then move on? Then I could taste the pleasure and not taste the sourness of the other aspects that you speak of.

"And the sweet memory I could keep."

"Perhaps. Maybe we could enjoy each other for a moment."

Yama touched my leg as she moved closer.

"You could have a glorious memory. Yet that memory will come between you and every woman you meet, for you will look at them as perhaps another chance of reliving being with me. Not to be bragging, of course.

"And if I turned out to be an unpleasant experience, for whatever reason, that memory will goad you on to hopefully find a better experience, while secretly you fearfully hope a repeat won't occur.

"Every lover will fail to satisfy because you have enshrouded them by your memories, instead of seeing each individual as a unique expression of the divine, because every memory is a lie to the present. And at some point with some woman, you will be pumping and grinding and the thought will arise as sharp as a meat cleaver: You are a liar and a cheat!"

"If I was single whom would I be cheating?" I asked.

"Truth.

"Though few know it, all are married to truth. Truth is our nature; it is our longing.

"Yet most sneak around thinking that truth sleeps, looking for some other lover. So many people slip into bed with another hoping to relive a moment or to invoke a fantasy from some romance novel or to feel good about oneself for being desirable or simply just to release some stress.

"And there is that little whisper: You cheat and lie!

"One can no more make love then can one make truth. Love is. Truth is.

"What can be made will be broken."

"I understand what you are saying, Yama," I said, my arousal diminishing but not completely.

"What if one is free from such desires and will occasionally have such interludes, just as one may occasionally drink a fine wine?"

I picked up my wine glass and took a long sip of the red wine.

"Do not fool yourself," Yama said, drinking from her glass, "most people go to bed with ghosts and phantoms of hope. Few see each other with the eyes of love.

"Besides, it is far safer drinking a glass of wine. To play with the fire of passion, one must reap the consequences.

"Sex is messy and so is its aftermath."

137

****

"You say sex is messy," I said. "Is not relationship messy as well? Who knows what to do in relationship anymore? Men are encouraged to be more nurturing, women are out of the homes providing the finances. The traditional roles are being turned upside down.

"What is the ideal relationship? Please help me in this. Though I seek the Self, I find myself again and again in a relationship with a woman."

"Beloved, there is no conflict in being in a relationship and seeking to know the Self. Relationship with a woman is but a means."

"But," I pleaded, "I do not want to be all strung out and caught in the web like all those we saw."

"To be caught in the web of relationship is when you see the relationship as an end, not as a means.

"Most children are trained, in one way or another, to get married, have children and prolong the family's name."

"What is the means then?"

"To share love.

"And to share love is to know love. For love is an action and not some thing to be had."

"How do you know when love becomes a thing?" I asked.

"A good measure to see how much of a thing love has become is the amount of drama to be found.

"When drama abounds you can be certain that both parties are caught in the web of you are supposed to do this and you are failing.

"Love makes no demands because it has nothing to gain.

"Only things can be added onto.

"Dramas are a drain. It is the ego's way of maintaining control. Control means fear. And fear keeps the ego alive.

"Especially in the West, where the individual personality is worshiped as the Self, the relationship, the marriage, will be substituted for the individual.

"As most personalities are self or ego-centered, so too do these relationships become self-centered and not Self or God-centered.

138

"There becomes a constant vying for control, of getting something out of the relationship, of maintaining the personalities."

"Then are you saying that an Eastern sort of marriage where tradition, and not personalities, dictate actions is better?" I asked.

"Who can say what is best for each soul. Both the West and the East offer a different learning experience.

"In a more traditional marriage, for instance, actions can become like learning by rote. This is how we do it because we have always done it that way. So that is what one does.

"There exists not much agony of choice as there is in the West where tradition is thrown out the window and everyone is standing on the edge of the unknown.

"Of course, in the more traditional setting less creative expression, fewer innovations, will arise as well. And the Soul can feel stifled."

"I would agree," I said. "I am a child of the West, my family scattered, doing their own thing, many divorces, separation. And it has been lonely at times, with the longing of a more traditional background.

"Yet when I see such a traditional marriage or family, I shudder at the thought of living in such a one.

"However, dramas do get old and that is what all my relationships have been. What can I do to end the drama?"

"Approach a relationship as you must approach all things. You are going to die. You are terminally ill with the disease of living in a body. Your time is short and precious.

"You do not have time to argue points, to barter favors, to demand, to submit.

"Act with assurance, the confidence, that there is no relationship to maintain.

"You are dying so how can you hold onto anyone? Give up dwelling on dramas. Focus only on Rama, only on God. It is not a coincidence that Rama is found in the word drama. If one sees only Rama dramas will not have such force to disturb one's peace of mind."

139

"Yama, if I acted as though I was dying might I not want to spend it with my loved ones and cut away what was not important?"

"Of course, if that is what you really wanted to do, what your heart bid you to do.

"The difference is that you are not working at making a successful marriage, you are not acting out of obligations, you are not doing anything then.

"You are simply acting out of Love.

"The problem with your relationship, and so many others, is trying to make these things work: Too much talk and seeking causes, and not enough listening; and far too much grasping.

"By knowing you are dying, the grasping falls away, love can be listened to much easier.

"And love is vast. Love is not confined to one's relationship or family. Love is an immense ripple, moving across the universe caused by the I AM.

"A healthy relationship is a reflection of the ripple, rippling out as an extension into the world.

"Love, my dear, may even ask you to leave a marriage."

"How does one know it is love and not fear? Fear of having to love one's spouse unconditionally, and wanting to just run away from all the pain of dealing and growing with another human being who comes with all their baggage?" I asked.

"When there is not drama. When calmness guides the action. Be fearless. You must be ready to cut away everyone, even your child, as the source of your happiness.

"Just as a soldier must leave his family to go and serve his country, or a doctor to leave her family at a moment's notice, so must you be ready to do so.

"After all, I am the ultimate summoner, and you cannot refuse my summons.

"A relationship to be healthy must extend into the world. When one is assisting in making the world a more beautiful, uplifting place, then one is working with mighty beings, ones who are working with the Soul of the World.

"Many families exist only for survival's sake, making sure there is enough food and adequate shelter, and when that is accomplished, to increase the family's comfort and opportunities for advancement.

"And these become little fiefdoms where loyalties and obligations hold prominence, and must not be broken.

"When a relationship is serving love and truth obligation and loyalty is reserved for God. Each partner must make contact with the silence within so that the other is seen not as someone who owes anything to the relationship, but as simply another aspect of God sharing a short time together."

"But what if you awaken to the desire to serve the world, and your partner, or your other family members for that matter, are focused only on the family and will not support what your heart bids you to do?" I asked. "What do you do then?"

"This may sound strange, but remember how that teacher was swallowed by the serpent because of the company he kept, surrounded by followers of the untruth?"

"Yes."

"Just because a person is in your family, whether of blood or by choice, does not oblige you to keep their company. If you have work to do to better the world, to better your Awareness of God and who you are, that you must do."

"No matter how loud the protestations?"

"No matter. This is where fearlessness comes in."

****

We sat in silence, sipping our wine, refilling our glasses. My glance occasionally strayed to the beauty of her form.

Yama said laughingly, "It's quite all right to delight in the beauty of this form, just as you would a flower or a gem. When you covet it though and want to possess it, then you will find yourself in trouble."

I laughed and raised my glass.

"Yama, you said that one does not need to be in the company of family if they are obstructing one's inner or outer work. Correct?"

"Yes, if you mean outer work that is directed by love for the betterment of the whole, not if it's for one's own ego gratification.

141

There are many a spouse who neglect others in their family because of their career ambitions, which do not help uplift the consciousness of the world."

"Let us say then that my partner is in some emotional upheaval; is it better for me to just walk out until the tempest passes?"

"Here is a suggestion. Before any tempest arise talk with your partner and form an agreement about what the two of you will do when a situation becomes painful, something like: When one is very upset acknowledge that the person has suffering and feels upset, and say that when calmness is restored you would be happy to hear the reason for the suffering. Otherwise by discussing it now, while suffering is prominent, only more suffering will ensue as most likely blame will be present and regrettable words spoken.

"And if your actions caused or triggered the upset and while you are listening you feel your emotions rise to a tempest, excuse yourself and say you will return when your awareness is not clouded by suffering."

"What if the other wants to hash it out right then and there?"

"Hopefully, there is the agreement the two of you had made to fall back on. Anyway, what do you care about most? Do you care more about maintaining the relationship or bringing Peace on earth?

"This is when fearlessness and calmness is needed to end a drama, by focusing on Rama. In dramas there is always pain, and there is far too much drama on this planet."

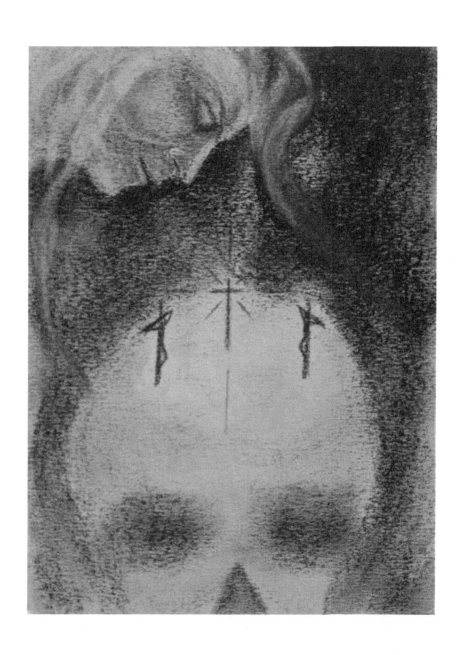

Chapter XXVII
Raising children; tradition of pain; changing tendencies; the crucifixion of the children; back to forgiveness; sanctuary for children; truth, beauty and goodness

143

We left the cafe after I paid for the drinks and we strolled down a busy, picturesque street. Yama took my arm and held onto it affectionately, turning my mind upside down. Not too long ago (although what is ago in dreams within dreams?) Yama was in the role of guru, now she (or he?) was walking with me as though she was a lover. I tried to watch my breath and not let my thoughts stray, lest Yama tune in on them. Yama laughed gently and playfully tapped my head.

"So many roles; so many forms. The poor mind gets so confused trying to make sense out of it all. Remember, there is only One, my beloved."

We came to a park and sat on the edge of a fountain and watched the passers-by.

"Thank you, dear Yama, for giving such wisdom on relationship. Now please tell me about the wisdom of raising children," I asked.

"So many times the gift of one's parents is to see what not to do; unfortunately, many will only bemoan their upbringing, not looking within themselves for the seed that brought such a childhood. So instead of learning from their parents' mistakes, they simply repeat them.

"And from generation to generation families are little more than television reruns.

"Look at that mother and child there."

I watched a young mother walking along side of her perhaps three-year-old daughter, the little girl licking her ice-cream cone with outright joy. Suddenly, the top of the cone fell off, right onto the girl's pretty blue dress, leaving a large white blotch.

"You stupid little girl!" the mother screamed in Italian, yanking her daughter's arm. "Why do I bother to make you look pretty?"

The girl whimpered as her mother viciously pulled her along in her anger.

We watched them disappear.

"The mother is doing the same thing her mother did to her and her grandmother did to her mother," Yama said. "If you make a mistake you will be punished and are not worthy of love is the message that each mother has taught, each of them thinking that

144

this is the proper way of raising children, creating generation after generation of fearful, creatively-deprived people, who call their lives living; yet, in fact, are nothing but involuntary reflexes of corpses."

"What about the little girl?" I asked. "Is there hope for her?"

"Somewhere along the family line one will come, who will break the sordid tradition. These are the ones who want the truth, to discover who they are and are not content with survival and comfort.

"These are the ones who will discover that they, too, have the poison within them and that they must draw it out. They must be vigilant and catch such a tendency immediately; or if it does occur through them to recognize the mistake and give it to God. And they need to apologize to the child or to whomever else they may have bitten."

"So a parent must be vigilant," I said.

"Yes. Parents are so often concerned about strangers molesting their children or about other dangers out there; instead, they need to be most vigilant with themselves."

****

Yama suddenly stood up. A fierce look came over her face. Her face began to change, turning black with rage. She grew in size. The park and the whole scene vanished. Her clothes ripped away revealing immense breasts and a pregnant stomach. She covered the sky.

Out of her vagina cherubs, winged chunky little babies of all races flew earthward. Light glowed around each. Their eyes shone. Their smiles like soft twilight.

Yet as they neared the earth, adults on the ground appeared, each holding a net. And like butterfly collectors they began to chase the cherubs, catching them in their nets.

The babies just smiled and cooed, radiating love. Until each one felt the nails driven into their hands and feet, impaled upon little crosses.

And the blood spurted. And the screams filled the air. And the Great Mother cried: No!

145

And the world looked nothing more than a graveyard of crucified babies, stretching farther than my vision could see.

I wept. I screamed.

I cursed for the children. I cursed for the Mother. I cursed for myself.

"Yama, let me not see this anymore!"

****

Yama now looked like my mother when I was a child. We stood in the living room where I grew up.

"Why are we here?" I asked, feeling apprehension in my gut.

"The suffering of the children must be seen. All save a few of my children are crucified. I feel every nail. And all the crucified children grow up, each carrying a mallet and nails.

"You are here, my child, to feel the nails and the pounding of the mallet so you will lay down your mallet and nails, that your son may grow up free of the cross.

Yama, my mother, beckoned me to lie down on the carpet. I obeyed, my heart pounding.

I am an infant, no, not even that, out of the warm dark I come, held firmly, squeezed, comforted. Then brightness shines through my eyelids. They open and sheering pain pierces my eyes from the metallic suns overhead. A man with a mask yanks me on high, holding my feet, meat on a hook, slaps my behind, and I wail, air rushing into lungs.

The nails go into my hands and feet.

I am on a cold table, an infant, my body wanting to curl as it did for all eternity in the warm dark. Only brightness here and the blazing light. Hands stretch my arms and legs.

Nails. Hands pull at what dangles between by legs, a flash of metal and pain, an eternity of pain between my legs, my whole being.

Nails.

Soft mounds and eyes aglow peering down. Warm milk flowing in my greedy mouth. Here is heaven. Eternal Bliss. All is well.

146

Body a little older. I want the soft mounds, cold rubber goes into my mouth. I turn my head. Still, those eyes gaze down at me. Only this rubber. I reach for the mounds. Hands pushed away. The rubber again. I turn. Hunger strong. Mouth on the rubber. It is not the same. The warmth of the womb missing from it. It is dead. The hunger. One more reach for the mounds. The rubber. I suckle. The hunger vanishes.

The nails pierce my flesh.

To walk. To reach. Hands and mouth one.

"No, not the vase!" The mallet.

"No, not the magazines!" The nails.

"No, not the stereo!" The pounding.

All that I reach for is all that I want to know, to become part of me. It is me. My world. Me. No difference.

Denied.

Cut away.

Dissected.

I sit down and cry.

Older now I sit in a desk. Many other children around me. A woman, my teacher, stands in front of the classroom, talking, talking, something about the importance of words and the sounds of the alphabet.

My body wants to run, to do, to swing, to jump.

I sit. I fade. The window beckons. The trees outside still, waiting to be climbed. I climb them in my mind. The teacher disappears. I am free!

Wham! A hand slaps my desk. I am torn from the trees.

"Daydreaming again!" her voice once more screaming. And her screaming turns into mine with the nails, with my screaming unheard.

I return home after school and my time with Nanny. "How was your day, honey?" my mother asks while my father pumps weights on the floor.

I want to tell them. I want to tell them every day. But I have learned. I do not want to be a failure when I grow up. I must say only good things.

"Fine," escapes from my mouth.

Nails.

The smoke goes into my lungs; soon the giggles and the munchies to follow. I pass the joint, and wash the smoke down with beer. I do not have too much time; lunch will soon be over. Dissecting frogs in my senior year will be more interesting today.

"How was school today, dear?" my mother asks, with the sounds of weights in the backyard.

"Fine, Mom."

"You are such a good boy. I'm so glad you haven't gotten in trouble like your older brother.

"Yes, Mom."

Nails.

****

"Enough!" I cried to Yama.

And the apartment, and my mother, and the sounding of the weights disappeared.

I hung on a cross on a rocky hill. Pain excruciating. Skulls and other human bones strewn about. To either side of me moaned a writhing man.

Yama stood below me, no longer looking like my mother; instead, he had changed back into the male form I was so familiar with. He gazed at me intently, and as I held his gaze his face changed once again. Now I stared into the eyes of my father.

"Father why have you forsaken me?"

I saw tears fall from his eyes.

"Have you not come to hammer more nails in?" I said accusingly

."No, my son. I would never knowingly hurt you. I've only done what I learned to do. These nails were simply my ignorance and my own crucified pain.

"Will you forgive me and let me remove these horrid nails, that there may be not nails that pierce your son's skin and all who come close to you, but nails that will build a placard that you will hold up, proclaiming that from these mistakes—my stakes—you will learn?"

I looked to either side of me. My neighbors were not strangers! Upon the crosses I saw my father and grandfather.

Yama in his familiar male form stood once more in front of me.

"Well," he said, "we are back here again, aren't we? Back to the place of forgiveness."

I weakly nodded.

"I forgive you, father," I said to him on my right.

"And," said Yama, "what do you proclaim?"

"I proclaim I will learn from his mistakes and be vigilant of such tendencies within me and to do otherwise to my son and others dear to me."

Yama lifted his hands to me.

"Then it is done."

****

I stood upon the ground next to Yama, looking at my now-empty cross. Then I saw my father still on the cross as well as my grandfather. I ran over to my father and reached up to pull out the nail binding his feet. Vainly I reached.

"Why is he still on the cross?" I shouted. "I forgave him. He should be down!"

Yama came over and put his hand on my shoulder. In his other hand he held one of the countless skulls.

"Your forgiveness has eased his pain. It is a balm for his suffering. But only he can take himself down, by forgiving his father, and his father his. And your forgiveness has shown him a pattern by which your father can forgive his father.

"All these skulls, my friend, are those throughout time, who chose suffering and death, and not forgiveness. And many have there been." No longer did we stand on rocky ground but on skulls. The whole hill was nothing save skulls. And high we stood above the plains.

"How many?" I gasped.

Yama shook his head and said, "Every star in the universe is but a beacon for every soul yet to forgive and to be a beacon for others."

Golgotha was no more. Instead, I, along with Yama, stood in a room covered with a soft red carpet. Wooden toys and wool dolls with featureless faces waited on the round-edged shelves. Colored silk hung from the windows and draped a table full of gnomes, rocks, acorns and flowers.

A silence, a hush, filled the room.

My heart began to stir as I picked up a wooden sword.

I wept not knowing why.

"What is this place?" I asked.

"This is a sanctuary for children. This is where children remember that truth, goodness, and beauty are the three pillars of the world.

"As young children want to consume the environment around them, here they are given a feast.

"Why the tears?"

"Because I know my soul craved to grow up in a school like this," I said.

"Yes, if a parent strives to have truth, beauty and goodness enrich the home and the lives of their children, and to find a school where these holy three are revered, then nails will be few."

"Please elaborate for I wish to spare my son the nails," I said.

"In the homes, in the schools, beauty is substituted for style. Style is flashy like a fishing lure. It seduces and quickly fades away. It fears to be caught naked without its make-up, lest it be discovered for the ugliness it truly is. Technology makes it glow.

"Beauty, on the other hand, grows with time and consciousness. Beauty is simple, nothing to flash, nothing to capture the eyes. It softly invites. Beauty clothes nature, and thus the more natural the more beautiful.

"Style arises from the mind.

"Beauty arises out of silence."

"Is not beauty in the eye of the beholder?" I asked."

Absolutely, one cannot see Beauty if beauty is not within the I. I am not speaking about the aesthetic details. Artists and philosophers and gardeners and poets and whoever else can argue until the end of time about such points, as to what colors go together, sentence structure, what flowers need to be planted where, etc. etc."

The Beauty I speak of encompasses the relative changing details, as the sky encompasses all things of the earth. It is a changeless beauty that quietly inspires, like a wisp of cloud upon granite peaks, or the moonlight shimmering in the surf, an old man taking the hand of a child who is lost. Beauty is the reminder of the Unity of All That Is."

"Tell me then of Goodness, Yama," I asked. "How does a parent bring Goodness into the home?"

"Notice the word that is found in the middle of the word home."

"O-M; OM!" I replied.

"Coincidence? Home is where the OM is. Where it is sacred, then there is home."

"However, is not OM everywhere? It pervades all, yes?"

"Just as everywhere on your mother was your mother, yet only from her breasts could you derive milk; so everywhere resounds the OM, but a home must be consciously created to make it a sacred place to nourish one's children.

"Peace and love must be the residing deities of the home. They must be looked to and consulted in all that the parents do. Objects must be seen as sacred and treated with respect, as well as the space within, keeping it free of chaos, to instill a peaceful mind.

"As the good sun rises each day in its rhythm, and the good moon changes with its time, and all things of nature behave according to the turning of the seasons, so too should a home have its rhythms.

"Just as soldiers will march against cannons moved by the beating of the drums, so too will it be easier when a routine is established to do what one needs to be done even when one is caught in a mood."

"For example, doing the dishes. If I have the habit of just doing them every night, then I do not have to think about doing them. I just do it," I said.

"Yes, when the children see the adults in the home establish habits, they too will develop them in themselves. Developing such habits will give them a discipline that they will carry throughout their lives and will make them less susceptible to the attack of moods."

"Should everything be in a routine then, like some military household?"

"Of course not. Moderation in all things, otherwise the routine becomes a god and a taskmaster and will not allow for the creativity of spontaneity."

"Please tell more about Goodness, teacher."

"Let your children see you helping, whether in the home or elsewhere. If they see their parents doing work that contributes to the uplifting of humanity and to the world around them, then the children will learn that they are part of the Whole and thus will feel whole as they grow up.

"If they just see parents only concerned about themselves and their family, ignoring the rest of the world, guarding their lot against loss, they will grow up with fear.

"If they see their parents looking outward and not family-absorbed, they will have a chance of creating relationships that are empowering instead of the usual me-me relationships."

"You have told me how Beauty and Goodness are needed to spare our children nails, now tell me about Truth and how that is helpful and can reside in the home."

"To invite truth into the home is to invite fearlessness. Especially as the child grows older and reaches the time of puberty, when their thinking capabilities blossom, they need to be allowed to question.

"If the parents and other adults in their lives show a flexibility of thinking, to look at an idea or a situation from a myriad ways, these children will not be simply unthinking fodder, manipulated by those in power.

"Such children will learn to question. Today in the homes and schools children are chained in obedience and force-fed facts. The children are given scriptures or history books or science books and are told to memorize them for they hold the truth.

"And all other ideas that oppose these views must be false.

"Their minds become programmed and they do not question their own mind.

"And they become trapped in their own mind box.

"To create an environment where perspectives from all sides are encouraged, an adult will be born who will be brave enough to even question the senses and even the mind."

****

We sat in silence awhile as I meditated on Yama's teachings.

"It is not easy to be a good parent and to raise children in a healthy way without hammering nails into them," I said.

"Indeed. Yet remember, you are not a parent but the Self expressing as a parent towards the Self expressing as your son.

"You must remember that so mistakes are allowed and guilt uninvited.

"All is well. Your son, like all children, will get everything they need. That which created All will take care of All."

"But why all the work, all the effort then?"

"Remember, the You who You are and who everyone is, is unaffected. If you see your son as flesh and bones you will only fear because then I have to come and do my work one day. What is born will die.

"See your son as he truly is and you free him from growing up in fear. To see him so you will see his radiant Beauty, you will do the greatest Good and you will stand in the Truth."

Chapter XXVIII
Following the heart; playing the Game; teaching

154

"Yama, I have a question," I said.

"Of course."

"You are in a male figure now and while traveling with you you have been male. Yet in the cafe and in the beginning of our journey you appeared in female form. Why? Are you more one form than the other?"

Yama laughed.

"I am neither male nor female. As well as I am both. I am not a vanishing body, whether a dream body or a physical one.

"My form is only in relationship to your beliefs. You see women, embodied by your earthly mother as generally more compassionate than men, and so when compassion is the lesson I may assume a female form. And in terms of trying to solve the mystery of relationship with women, who better but a woman could answer such questions."

"Yet, overall, you see men as the great teachers and you so long to look up to a male as the embodiment of truth. Therefore I have chosen a male form."

"Why do I long to seek a male teacher so?"

Yama leaned over to me and jabbed his finger in my forehead.

"Because, my friend, you do not see yourself as embodying the truth. Thus you need a mirror.

"The teacher is nothing but a mirror reflecting what you already know.

"Your first male teacher, your father, did not embody the truth; instead he was caught in the ways of his father and the world. Then you came across other teachers fooled by powers and wrapped in delusions of specialness. Now you seek a male teacher who will not fail your expectations of perfection; so that you may at last see perfection in yourself.

"Yet it is a ploy."

"What do you mean that it's a ploy?" I asked, feeling the commencement of the build up of walls.

"You will never find a perfect teacher," Yama replied. "Search and do not find. If you did find a perfect teacher then you would see yourself, and know that a true teacher was possible."

"So?" I said.

"What do you want to do with your life? I mean, really want to do?"

"To find the truth."

"That has nothing to do with doing. Finding the truth is not about doing at all. Truth is here. You are already That. Finding the truth is knowing it.

"I'm talking about doing, having the Self express through you as a unique expression of consciousness."

"How can I know that? Is not such a desire born of delusion, fabricated by the mind wanting to keep me in the world, in its power?"

"You have asked about parenting. This is a lesson in parenting."

"In parenting? You are not asking about my son; you are asking about what I want to do?"

"To act as the best parent is to do what your heart, consciousness, moving through you as a unique expression, bids you to do.

"Desire is to sire, to give birth. You, my student, are pregnant. If you abort the desire within you you will show your son that the will of God is meaningless, and not worthy of giving it life, expression.

"Give it birth and you show your son that God's Will, Dharma, is worth the risk and pain of labor.

"So I ask you again: What is the secret labor of your heart?"

With those last words he placed his hand on the middle of my chest. And with his touch came a rush of emotions.

"How do I know if this desire is from God or from the ego?" I pleaded.

"Come, I will take you to a place where it is easier to know. Just as in this room, where Goodness, Truth, and Beauty reside, to nourish the children to grow into powerful, loving, wise, creative adults, so too if a desire wants to be born and Goodness, Truth and Beauty can guide it and nourish it, then it is a desire from the heart.

"If the desire promotes selfishness, egotism, arrogance, dependency, deceit, and greed, know it rises from the ego."

"But what if the desire contains both? The desire that arises within me I can see all such qualities, or at least potential."

156

"You need to look at the desire separately. Just as wanting and raising a child can be a mixture of altruism and selfishness; yet the desire to raise a child is a desire born of Goodness, Truth, and Beauty. That desire to bring children in the world is a part of the flow of all things.

"It is in harmony. And harmony is God's will."

****

We stood on the shore of a quiet lake, conifer trees lined the hills surrounding the water, like a living bowl. Quiet reigned. Even though crows and jays croaked and shrilled.

"Why do not the cries of crows and the jays, which are far from the beautiful sounds of the songbirds, do not disturb the silence around?" I asked.

"Because nature is the desire of God. The desire within your heart is no different.

"Your faults and human weaknesses are no more than crows and jays. They are not You; they are not the desire.

"Focus on the desire and on the Self from which the desire appears to arise, and listen, with humor, to the squawks and shrills."

"Why do you say, appears to arise?" I asked.

"Because there exists nothing outside the Self. The Self encompasses all. Because we are speaking and using cumbersome words that differentiate, we speak of desire and Self as two. But there is no two. Always remember That."

"Now look at that heron over there wading amongst the water plants. What do you observe?"

"It moves silently and slowly with extreme concentration. It is vigilant of both what it seeks and the dangers around," I said.

The heron stopped and became as still as the trees around. For a long while we watched. Then in a flash and a splash a fish flopped a moment in the bird's beak, before disappearing down the heron's throat.

"What else?" asked Yama.

"Extreme patience. Stillness. Swiftness and certainty. Firm hold. Swallowing. Calmness. Then back to stillness."

157

"You have described desire born of the Heart and how to manifest it.

"Out of silence the desire arises. When it arises there is a calmness and patience in waiting for its fulfillment.

"To fulfill it concentration is needed, one-pointed focus; while at the same time vigilance of any fears and doubts, arrogance and greed, and especially impatience.

"Remembering all the while the silence and to be still as a stone within, not to become excited at the prospect of fulfillment, nor anxious of its possible failure.

"And when the opportunity arises for the desire's realization, act and act swiftly, holding on firmly.

"And when it is accomplished enjoy it and let it pass. And wait in the silence for another desire to arise out of the silence."

****

"So tell me, what desire lies buried in your heart that wants to be born before I come to you as death?

"Remember, your body is dying. You are terminally ill as all are on this planet. When you are dying petty things lose their significance and only the essential remains."

"Yama, you the Great Reminder, I look around the world of waking consciousness and see so many teachers teaching about how to know God or to know the Self; while they are soaking in a stew of egotism.

"I had a dream where I stood with Jesus in front of the masses in Constantinople, and he spoke to them. Then I stood and spoke, he speaking through me and I said,

"You do not need anyone to tell you what is true. The truth lies within your heart.

"And the crowd replied, Yes, you are wise. Be the bishop of the new church.

"No! I said. You do not need anyone to tell you what is true!

"They would not listen and I awoke in tears."

"Yet...?" pried Yama.

158

"I want to teach. I want to teach not only little children but adults as well. I want to be a guide to inspire, to encourage others to find the truth of who they are.

"Yet I recall the temple and the snakes and the goo-goo eyes of the followers, and I am terrified. I do not want to be a guru that people follow blindly and wait outside my toilet. I have too many imperfections to be seen as such a one. My heroes in stories have been those mysterious guides who come just when the hero is lost. Yes, I want to be only a guide who is on his own journey, hopefully passing on pearls of wisdom to others on theirs.

"But what if I fall? What if I advise someone with counsel that is appropriate for me and not for them and mess up their journey? Or what if I do not live always by what I preach and become nothing more than a hypocrite?"

Yama smiled and said, "What would you do if you knew that you could not fail; that, in fact, life was an experiment and that God was asking you to take risks so He has something to work with?

"What if no one had ever taken a risk, what the hell kind of story would this Game be? And anyway, who is it that thinks he is doing anything anyway? Only the ego. God is doing it all. You just need to pretend you are actually doing something.

"You strut around teaching those close to you anyhow. Just go out and stick your head on the block."

"But what about the dream with Jesus?"

"That is the paradox: In truth there is no teacher or student. Yet in duality God is always sending teachers or guides. And the desire to be a teacher is a desire in harmony because, like the desire for children is needed to continue the species, teachers are needed to continue humanity's growing awareness and to help one another on the search for truth.

"However, with more knowledge gained, one has the responsibility to give advice only when asked. Otherwise, in a manner, one may be interfering with another's destiny.

"Regardless, just as the children you instruct teach you, so will the adults who will come teach you quite a lot about yourself."

"I think that is what I am afraid of."

Chapter XXIX
Creativity; the 3-fold path' the final revelation of Yama

"There is another doubt I see squawking in your mind," Yama said, eying me like the crow in the tree.

"Yama, you have shown me that knowing the Self, the Changeless state of Being is all important, that anything else is a distraction. However, I am an artist as well. Where does creativity come into play, or is it just like allowing the general of the mind to come into the trenches and take charge?

"Please clarify this point, for my heart is in anguish at the thought of not creating."

"You ask, 'Where does creativity come into play?'

"That is the answer."

"What is the answer? Mine was a question!"

"Creativity is the Play. The Creator creates. It is the act of consciousness.

"Consciousness is the Mind of God, creating the world's Drama.

"Tell me, do you think, do you engage your mind when you are in the flow of creating?"

"No, not at all. I lose my sense of time, of me. Only when I think about whether people will like my work, how much I may sell the piece for, and other such thoughts, does the mind kick in."

"Sit down and watch your breath and tell me what you observe."

I sat awhile on the beach of the lake, eyes closed, watching, breathing. With eyes still closed I said, "I inhale. A slight retention. Exhalation. And then back again."

"Very good. Now you have described your path. It is an ancient path, though you will give it your own twist because of your culture and era.

"Nothing in this world is Real. Nothing out there will bring you Happiness. Withdraw your breath from the world.

"This is the truth and the first step. Back to being-ness. The I before the I. Only God, the imperishable, the changeless, the Self, is real. Only That which is within can offer happiness.

"Retain that breath. Hold it for the preciousness that it is. This is the second step.

161

"Enjoy the beauty, the love, that awaits within. Awareness of the I AM, of the Beloved. Hear the wondrous beating of the heart and the silent hum of the eternal.

"And finally, the last step is that all the world is God.

"There exists nothing apart from the Self. All is you. Happiness exists everywhere.

"Exhale and see all as God. Enjoy the goodness of creation, of creating. Create, create, create. Exhale into the world just as the Creator exhales his children into existence, who are born to remind the dead how to play once again. This is consciousness at play.

"Being.

"Awareness.

"Consciousness.

"Dear child, you who asked for nothing but the truth at the beginning of this dream when you inquired about who I was, I will now reveal to you who I am.

"My name is Yama. Yet before I was named I was. That being has never ended. Awareness of my being still exists, and this unique form of consciousness plays its part as death and Dharma.

"Behold."

Suddenly a flash of light replaced the form of Yama. I raised my hands before my eyes, warding off the brilliance. The Mighty OM issued forth before me, echoing within me.

The light began to fade to a bearable level. Standing before me he stood. I fell to the ground and touched his feet.

Three heads radiated light upon his shoulders. His head on the left had long black hair, in which a crescent moon shone. The center head wore a golden crown and golden earrings and a necklace. And the head on the right had long thick white hair and beard.

Each head was radiantly beautiful.

All the heads spoke as One.

"In one tradition I am Shiva, the Destroyer, attached to nothing of the world, leading all to the One Being. I am the embodiment of wisdom. I am the Father. I am the Crone. I am dispassion and discrimination. I lead all to the truth eternal by cutting away all the perishable.

"I am Vishnu, the One who preserves all that is done with love. I am the Holy Spirit. I am the Mother. I am the beauty in the world. I am love and live as compassion in the hearts of all. I am the bridge as I am aware of all that exists in heaven. I am devotion.

"I am Brahma. Just as without the sun nothing could live upon the earth, so too without my creative force nothing could be. I am the Son. I am the Maiden. I am the embodiment of creativity itself. I am the consciousness of all beings evolving, expanding. I make the world a better place by inspiring humans to serve another. I am creative action. I am Dharma.

"We are the Three that is One.

"Do you know why you can behold us?"

I could say nothing. Only tears fell in response.

"You can only behold that which you can recognize, and you can only recognize that which is within you.

"Just as one who is truthful can recognize the truth, one who is loving can perceive love and one who does good can choose good.

"You, like all your brothers and sisters, are divine. You have always been so and will always remain so.

"We are you.

"You are That which you seek.

"Rise."

I arose. My whole being vibrating, resonating with the one OM. Only the OM.

"Come," said Yama, holding out his arms. The Three now looking as the one I had known.

I walked. OM. Into his arms.

"Be what you have sought."

No arms held me. No arms existed and no me.

OM.

Only OM

And then it happened.

I awoke.

I AM

And I dreamt ... .

Addendum I
The Ten Commandments: A Nondualism Perspective

The following story/teaching/conversation originally appeared in six parts starting in the Summer Edition 2005 of Pathways Within. It looks at the Ten Commandments, not as absolutes, but as guidelines to come to place of unity and place of enlightenment.

The sound of waves crashing became louder as we walked through the sparse coastal woods. Then we broke free of the trees and found ourselves walking by the steep cliffs. Thousands of sea birds jostled and squawked on the nearby rocky islands. Yama and I sat down on a bench and watched in silence awhile.

DISCIPLE: Yama

YAMA: Yes?

DISCIPLE: Why do you walk with me?

YAMA: I walk with everyone; it's just that most people don't want to remember that. They are hoping I am far away. Because of your meditation practice of cutting away all that is transitory you have found the wisdom to face the fact of your body's mortality.

I kept silent and watched an otter smash an urchin with a stone and gobble up the meat inside.

DISCIPLE: You have talked about the need for us to become human, that just because we have a human body there is still a lot of work to do. For most of us we struggle between following our instincts, which consists of basic survival needs or chasing after the pleasing and running from the painful, and this inner urge to find ultimate freedom where we are not caged by time and space, or more importantly, caught in the snares of identifying one's Self with the body or mind.

YAMA: Yes?

164

DISCIPLE: Well, I was just reading the Bible and came across the Ten Commandments that God gave Moses, as well as the manifold rules the Israelites were commanded to observe. I see nothing freeing in such edicts; in fact, I find them suffocating. I would rather die than live under such restrictions. Jails, for goodness sake, offer more freedom!

Yama laughed.

YAMA: Talking like that in times past would have given you a great collection of stones!

General rules can be very tricky, for everybody has their own path in the end. However, in the beginning, just as in school, groups of souls will have general lessons to learn and master before moving to the next grade. Then there is graduation and all the members of the group go their separate ways, with Life giving each an abundance of lessons unique to their own learning needs.

The Ten Commandments were such a group lesson plan, helping to mold a race of people for specific reasons for the body of humanity. However, there exist different levels of understanding as well, from gross to subtle. Just as the poet may sing about becoming drunk with the wine of love, some will take that as the partaking in the sensual pleasures of the body, while another will see it as a call for drinking in the sweetness of devotion for God.

DISCIPLE: Please elaborate. I seek to understand the subtlest form of truth.

YAMA: Then listen with your heart, and feel it as a breeze of knowing.

What is the First Commandment?

DISCIPLE: You shall have no God other than me. Now, I have statues of Shiva and Ganesh and chant names of gods of many traditions. Would this be considered a sin?

YAMA: If you see God as a force outside of you then there will be conflict. But if you see God, the I AM THAT I AM, which is the Holy Name of Jehovah, as both within and without, that everything is included in God, and that God moves through all things, whether the gross things of the world or through the subtle worlds and their denizens, including the gods, then everything becomes an expression of God, with none able to represent the ineffable quality of God. For instance, Shiva is an expression of God to remind us to not be attached to any form, to go deep into the Infinite Self, or the I AM THAT I AM; Vishnu is that form of expression to uphold the good and the beautiful, and to inspire devotion; and Brahma is that aspect that shows the creative dynamic quality of the Divine. Yet all of them are simply one of the million faces of Brahman, the formless, the changeless.

In other words, if you think that any form of God is the true form than that is ignorance. There is no separation between you and God since God is everywhere, including yourself. Even though sometimes even I have a hard time believing my last statement is true.

He smiled.

YAMA: Next.

DISCIPLE: Well the next one states that we should not make any images of anything created, whether in heaven or on earth. And if there are any images created then there shall be no worshipping of these images because God is a jealous god. Well, I am guilty of this in a big way, as are most artists, not to mention a whole host of religions. From what you said about not seeing God as outside my Self, then I can understand that I should not worship any image outside of me. Yet, what of the first part of the rule?

YAMA: This was an edict specific for the followers of Moses to counter the traditions of the other religions in the region who worshiped images of gods, and who even sacrificed to them. These idol worshipers actually believed that these gods were separate from themselves and not an aspect of the one Mind of

Consciousness. Buddhists, for instance, use statues of the Buddha, or of various deities, not to propitiate but to meditate upon to bring such qualities through them. They are viewed as qualities of Mind. To see the stillness of the statue of a Buddha reminds one to find the calmness within. Another point is that no matter how one paints the world one can never show the truth of what anything is. To place an image of a man on the cross can only convey a small fraction of who Jesus is or what he did. But if someone says that one must worship that image to worship Jesus, than that is just ignorance. The Navaho and Tibetan Buddhists will create sand paintings, spending a long time with each piece. And when it is done either they wipe it away with a stroke of the hand as with the latter, or let the wind blow it away. In this way there is no grasping of the image as real, but only as a means of focus. Nothing more than a beautiful thought.

The Truth is jealous. You can only worship the Infinite or the finite. If you focus on one the other goes to the background. If you worship the Infinite than all the finite is naturally included. God or mammon.

DISCIPLE: Thank you. The third I recall is about not saying God's name in vain. Please elaborate.

YAMA: Your scientists are slowly discovering that everything vibrates. Sounds create forms. In the Bible Joshua destroyed the walls of Jericho through the power of sound. The walls of ignorance can equally be knocked down by the Name of God.

DISCIPLE: Well what is the true Name of God?

YAMA: Just as you are called by many names so too is God. Now your wife can call you one thing and your son another. You will answer to both. The problem comes when others might hear one of them calling you and see you answer. Then they run off to their people and say that your name is Honey Dear. But others who had heard your son address you will go to their camp and say you are called Pops. Debates ensue. Passions get heated. Wars begin. Saying a Name of God as the one Name is vanity and will not bring the desired effects of knocking down the walls of the ego because it is the ego which is now manipulating the use to create confusion and division. You can rest assured that when the mind shouts: I know the Answer. I know the Truth. It is nothing but ego. Truth is very humble.

DISCIPLE: Then how should one speak a holy Name?

YAMA: With reverence, because not only are you reminding yourself that there exists a Power way beyond the little thing you believe you are, but one is actually affecting both subtle and physical matter. Today scientists can show actual forms created by various sounds. Or even by thought, which is a more subtle form of sound. Quantum physics shows that the viewer affects the subjects viewed through preconceived ideas. Sound and thought are condensed ideas. Chanting Holy Names and mantras vibrate one's self and the world (which is only natural if you know that there is only the One). This is why one's speech and thoughts are so important and one must be vigilant of every word and thought, since these are what are vibrating one's world.

We returned to the silence as I wanted to take in what my guide had said before continuing. The waves crashed amongst the cliffs below in thunderous claps. It seemed the whole earth rattled with each wave, just as a lover shivers with the touch of his beloved. The silence and the waves, the bench and my body—the boundaries disappeared.

****

Yama and I left the crashing of the waves of the coastal sanctuary and made our way to the nearby mission. No one else sat amongst the pews of the chapel on this week day; thus were we safe from the tourists who buzzed about in groups listening to the one-sided historical views of tour guides and how the Native peoples were given a better life by the coming of the Spaniards. In contrast to the heat outside, the air in the chapel felt cool to my body and soul.

DISCIPLE: Yama, you have elaborated on three of the Ten Commandments. You have said that there exists different levels of understanding to all teachings and that these commandments are no different. As I said before when I take the Commandments literally I find them restrictive to the expansiveness of my soul; yet hearing your words I am beginning to find in them much wisdom. Please continue with my lesson.

YAMA: Remember that every moment and every place has lessons with many levels. Behold this place where both the blood of those enslaved by fellow human beings was spilt and the blood of the Great Master was taken that gave many a peace beyond the physical conditions. No matter what the historical views one might have they are only selective by what is deemed believable, that is why historical debates will always be pointless in the end. However, if one just sits with a still mind, existing between breaths, one will come to the Truth behind all actions.

With that said, tell me of the Fourth Commandment.

DISCIPLE: To remember the Sabbath day and keep it holy. God took a day off after creating for six days so we should as well, including our servants and animals which toil for us. Now I know there are many interpretations of what resting means and what day of the week is the Sabbath. So what is the truth?

YAMA: Just as holidays, or Holy Days, are created to remind people that there is more to life than just going about and doing things, or providing for one's family and increasing one's profit, so too must time be set aside for quiet reflection. Take for example those passing through these grounds today. They are busy listening to someone telling them their interpretation about the truth of this place, hearing a bunch of facts, and seeing objects wrapped in stories. It does not matter that they may be on vacation from their daily work; their minds are still working, weaving together a limited picture of their experience here. Their minds goad them on to find out more, to become educated about the history of this mission, driving them onward and keeping them from discovering this inner chapel. For here the mind is threatened. For here the mind confronts the Silence that it cannot understand.

If one is doing work that keeps the mind active and does not engage the heart then time is needed to be set aside to go to the Silence beyond the mind, where the Holiest of Holies resides, the I AM THAT I AM. This is the condition of most humans who work to survive or to better the condition of themselves and their families. And each day their Awareness of their infinite nature becomes more veiled.

However, for those who keep their mind trained to reside in the Silence, to keep it focused on God, who do work that allows for the expression of the heart and helps to uplift their fellow human beings and to make this world a better place without the concept of "I am doing this or that," then every day and every moment is holy and thus the Sabbath is kept continually.

DISCIPLE: So setting time aside each day you would consider as keeping with this injunction, yes?

YAMA: Absolutely, the society in which you live in needs much help in setting quiet time aside from all the business. And this quiet time does not include entertainment. While entertainment is a rest of sorts and has its place for relaxation, it can still be a distraction for the mind to further engage in. It is to reside in the Silence that makes any moment holy.

DISCIPLE: What about engaging in the arts, whether listening to music or going to a museum, or doing artistic activities, as well as reading sacred works, would these constitute rest?

YAMA: On one level all said activities can lift one out of the daily toil of doing, or they may not. If the mind is spinning on any of these activities, thinking about this or that one instant and thinking about something else the next, not being focused on what is at hand, then it is more toiling. And if there is a sense of I am doing this or reading that, which maintains the ego's view that the Self is the body and not the timeless Self that we really are, which includes but is untouched by the actions of the body, then it is nothing but more ignorance. And being of ignorance then where is Truth? And if Truth is missing then so is God.

DISCIPLE: How can one tell if one is acting without thinking?

YAMA: If you are at rest. The body at the end of the day or week may be exhausted if there has been physical labor, or the mind may be tired if mental activities have been prevalent, but none of that fatigue touches the sense of I. In a person who remembers one's Self stress will not be present. For the Self is the power behind the activities of the mind and the body, just as the sun is untouched by all actions on the earth, although without it, life could not exist.

The Fifth Commandment?

DISCIPLE: Honor thy father and thy mother so that one's days are long upon the earth.

YAMA: There are two levels I will speak upon. The first is the material level that is a reminder that without your mother and father you would not be here; at least in the form that you find yourself in. Your parents have not only given you a portal in which to come into this world, both of them have colored you by each of their hereditary lines or the spirits of their ancestors.

DISCIPLE: I am not sure if that is a good thing when you look at some of my ancestors.

YAMA: It is neither good nor bad. It simply is. Whether you like it or not the actions of your ancestors have had an influence on you.

DISCIPLE: How?

YAMA: Your great grandfather, for example, had a very cold, removed personality who gave corporeal punishment as a way to mold the behavior of his son, your grandfather. This manner of expression your great grandfather passed on to his son and he passed it on to his—your father. You grew up in such conditions.

DISCIPLE: Yeah, but I do not have to pass it on.

YAMA: Only if you honor your father.

DISCIPLE: Why should I honor him? He doesn't even speak to me.

YAMA: Honoring does not mean to like what the person does, but to see them in high regard.

DISCIPLE: How can I see him or anyone in high regard if their actions do not warrant it? That's ridiculous.

Yama smiled and pointed to the crucifix on the wall, where Jesus has hung in agony for hundreds of years.

YAMA: Do you think Jesus liked what his people did?

DISCIPLE: No.

YAMA: Do you doubt that he not only honored the people who put him upon the cross, but his Father as well, by whose Will caused the crucifixion to occur as well?

DISCIPLE: No.

YAMA: So it is with your earthly father. Without him you would not have learned many of the lessons you have learned nor be the person you are today. To honor thy father and mother it is to look beyond their actions to the Eternal Father/Mother where we all arise and reside within. Can you find any positive traits that your father has manifested?

I nodded my head.

DISCIPLE: Many.

YAMA: If you can focus on those traits you will honor your father and those positive traits, which are seeds, will continue to grow and manifest in you. And those traits that have been as a poison to you, thank him for showing you what not to do and to give you a challenge to overcome. For without a challenge one's soul does not grow. Believe me, if you had found yourself in the household that you think you should have been brought up in you would have grown weak in many ways.

This holds true with your mother as well. One cannot honor one parent and dishonor the other if one wants to live fully on this earth. Both the masculine and the feminine must be equally embraced or one will not go forward, but will go in a circle, like a cart with one wheel not working. Everyone has their parents living in them.

DISCIPLE: I hear you Yama about honoring the gifts of my parents, both the pleasant and the bitter ones. However, what about when one begins to be an adult and your parents tell you to do one thing but your heart tells you to do what they are forbidding you to do. To whom does one listen?

YAMA: To listen to your heart, is to listen to me as Dharma, reminding you that your time on earth is coming to a close and thus you must act accordingly. Will you have regrets for what you did not do when I come as death? And for that matter, for what you did do? With that in mind, who holds more weight in the scheme of things: your parents or Dharma?

DISCIPLE: Dharma, of course. For Dharma is Eternal. Even the gods must follow Dharma.

YAMA: Then that is your answer. In truth, by following your Dharma you honor your parents, although they most likely will not tell you so. Yet there comes a time when a parent's role is that of the guardian of the threshold. They are a test, telling you that you must go the other way while their soul wants you to pass through them.

DISCIPLE: Is that why Jesus said that we must say goodbye to our families if we were to follow him?

YAMA: Yes, for he was speaking as the Living Truth, and not as a personality. With each moment one must think of following Truth and not the dictates of the material needs of survival. If one lives by survival needs then one believes he is a body and surely death will come soon enough. But if one follows the quest for Truth in each moment there exists only the Eternal.

DISCIPLE: Well I have a family to feed. By going to work and providing for my family, am I then not following Dharma?

YAMA: As long as the work is such that when you die and you watch the movie of your experiences on earth you are not going to wince and cover your eyes. In other words you will have no regrets about your actions.

I was about ready to raise another question when Yama motioned me to silence. He reached over and tapped my chest.

YAMA: Here is the place, beyond all the ranting of thoughts, that calls for your mind to come and rest within.

A vibration filled my being. I felt like my body was a buzz of atoms spinning around and keeping a tentative form, like an oscillating cloud of gnats. My eyes fell shut. My thoughts disappeared. Even the thought of searching for thoughts I could not create. I looked for the source of me but I could not find any specific place. Only an Awareness existed and I was That....

****

Yama and I sat in the cemetery overlooking the ocean, a golf course on three sides. On this sunny, cool day the links were filled with people hitting little balls into holes, no doubt ignoring the mortality reminders a chip away, while the murder of crows in the cypress trees that provided shade for the graves, cawed for the golfers' attention.

DISCIPLE: It has been a long time since our last discussion about the more non-dualistic interpretation of the Ten Commandments.

YAMA: Has it? Do not your dreams jump from scene to scene, with what seems like much time between them, all of which happens within a few breaths of "real" time?

DISCIPLE: Yes, that's true.

YAMA: So it is with me. Our last conversation was just a moment ago, since I am not bound by time, and thus do not use it as a reference of who I am. My reference point is with the Eternal so I am not defined by what I do, even though my role is death.

DISCIPLE: Well that brings us to the Sixth Commandment: Thou shall not kill. As death, are you not the greatest offender of this rule?

YAMA: I guess I am; but then so must God be, for my power comes from Her. However, can God kill anything since all things abide in God and God in all things? Right here is the whole rub because when we get to the Essential, which is God, that there is only One. Yet it takes two to have the play of killer and slain.

This is what Krishna said to the warrior Arjuna who didn't want to fight his kinsmen. Krishna reminded him that the Eternal Self cannot kill or be slain, and that everybody is just passing phenomena being consumed by time under the control of God.

Really the commandment should say: Thou cannot kill.

DISCIPLE: Ok, what you say I understand to mean that finite occurrences do not affect the Infinite Source, no more than my throwing a pebble in the ocean can disturb the depths.

YAMA: Well put.

DISCIPLE: Yet it does say, 'shall not kill,' as an injunction for right living in accord with God's will. What does it mean? Surely it doesn't mean that humans should not kill one another because immediately after giving the commandments to Moses, Jehovah has Moses put to death thousands of idol worshipers.

I am confused.

YAMA: Such is the problem when one lives according to the words of another, because everyone comes to words with subjective interpretations. All teachings will appear to have contradictions because no matter how holy they are they basically are nothing more than ripples on the ocean. Words are expressed in time and Truth is Eternal and the two can never meet.

Some will say it means to kill no human being, that one should prefer to die than to kill. Others might say it means to kill nothing at all, if at all possible—which I assure you it is not. Others talk about just wars, and say it is legitimate to kill when defending one's home or country. And then there is the eye for an eye permission.

Which interpretation is right? Which one wrong? When one realizes that there is no other, no thing or person out there to be feared, that the Self is only One, one will act in harmony with the Whole. In such a case, then one may be the instrument of helping a finite form change as it inevitably will, just as the surgeon removes a tumor or the general defeats the invaders, the butcher prepares the cow for a feast. Some may even feel that by self immolation they can kill the flames of war.

DISCIPLE: So you are saying that there really is no absolute to this rule?

YAMA: Yes, except only that you can't kill. Jesus knew this very well when he asked God's forgiveness for those who knew not what they were doing, because their ignorance saw them killing Jesus. But how can the Eternal Son of God be killed? Of course God forgave them because His Son never died.

DISCIPLE: Here we sit in a graveyard. Is there any point to such a place if nobody dies?

YAMA: Such memorials are at best good reminders that bodies eventually drop away, to help people wake up to their nature and to

176

remind them not to become attached to anything or anyone, for all things pass away. Cemeteries can indeed be a good place to meditate for those reasons. However, as a place to dwell on the memories of those who passed, it can keep people's minds stuck in time. Really, people should have memorials for clothes they can no longer fit into, it makes about as much sense, for the body is but a garment. Besides, people put too much emphasis on memories, thinking that they are what makes them who they are. Memories are simply thoughts, and one's Self rests quietly beyond them.

With that last thought in mind we watched the crows silently before closing my eyes, eliminating everything that I call mine from me: my family, my things, my work, my body, my personality, my feelings, my thoughts...until no thing was left. And only Silence remained.

****

Yama and I sat on a park bench overlooking the bay of Monterey, right next to the bike path where scantily clad women ran under a sun long hidden. Often my eyes would stray down the path instead of watching the otters or the seals down below.

DISCIPLE: Yama, I am a married man, and very happily so; yet my eyes wander over the beauty of the female form, and if I am not vigilant my mind will conjure up some wanton fantasy in the blink of an eye. The Seventh Commandment is: Thou shall not commit adultery. Am I committing adultery with my thoughts? And what is the highest teaching of this commandment?

YAMA: Adultery by definition is the sexual union of a married man or woman with another person outside of marriage. While God does not care one whit what you do in time, as God sees only the Eternal and sees no other; however, as a discipline for one who seeks to know God or one's own true nature, then one needs to cull the panting after forms—however beautiful they may seem to be. After all, what are these forms anyway but decaying flesh, one moment youthful and beautiful, the next withering and decrepit. Or if one explores these bodies further by looking at them at the

177

minutest level they are nothing but particles of energy with no solidity at all.

Running after a body for a moment of pleasure is like jumping into the desert sand after believing you saw water. Bodies can no more give you happiness than mirages can quench your thirst.

DISCIPLE: But what about thinking about it? It's not quite as bad, is it?

YAMA: Finding yourself in bed with some woman other than your wife would have been perpetuated by your thinking; it is not the body that wants to be with another body. When your consciousness leaves your body the body becomes inert, such as in deep sleep. The body is neutral, but it is filled with mental tendencies. If you have a habit of wanting to enjoy every pretty body, then a subconscious tendency will be created by the belief that such actions will bring fulfillment. And each time that tendency is acted upon it reinforces that notion. Therefore, the mind is the one that needs to be controlled by not letting it wander after the temporal. This is where discrimination is so important.

DISCIPLE: Please elaborate about discrimination.

YAMA: Does a wise man choose to pursue something that holds it value throughout time or something that has a value that will last only a day?

DISCIPLE: Obviously only the former. Only a fool would spend time and resources chasing something that is only valuable for a day.

YAMA: So discrimination is choosing between what is truly valuable and what is not. That which is Eternal has everlasting value. Anything temporal is really valueless. And the mind only focuses on what one believes is valuable. A business man will focus on profit, a drunk on his booze, a doctor on her patients, a holy man on God.

DISCIPLE: Is therefore my marriage valueless? And if it is, why not go after any women I wanted?

YAMA: It is valueless if you think your wife will complete your life for you and if you see her as a body. A marriage is only valuable in the true sense that it offers an opportunity of expressing unconditional love towards someone you see on a daily basis— someone whom you can see every shortcoming and then look beyond to her radiant perfect Self. Marriage is a powerful tool to discover unlimited joy in a limiting framework; which is no different than anything else on this planet.

And like everything else on this planet marriage is simply a mirror. If you see your wife as a body floundering in time and space then that is what you will see yourself as. If you behold her as the Christ, so shall you see yourself.

In other words, the only worthy undertaking is to find the Eternal in the finite.

DISCIPLE: In truth then, adultery does not just entail not lusting after someone else for sexual pleasures, but may encompass other areas as well.

YAMA: Certainly. There are many ways for one to want to escape the lessons of marriage, whether it is through one's work, socializing, watching television, reading, etc.

DISCIPLE: Well, I do all those things from time to time. So am I escaping my marriage through them?

YAMA: You can tell if you are having an affair with anything if your mind fixates on having them when you are in another activity. If you are walking with your wife and your mind dwells on the book you are reading, or if your are doing the dishes and you want to be out with your buddies, then you are not present.

Remember this teaching: that one is to be married, not to a human being, but to the Eternal Now, to God, and when one's mind is focused on anywhere else other than where one is at the time, this is adultery.

DISCIPLE: Thank you for giving me your commentary on adultery. I realize now that one does not have to be married to commit adultery. And my wandering eye is simply the mind wanting me to not be content with where I am and with whom I live.

We sat still awhile, this time I was completely focused on the harbor seals lying motionless sunbathing on the rocks, these marine creatures being very hard to distinguish from the stone they lay upon.

DISCIPLE: "Thou shall not steal" is the next commandment. It seems simple enough. Anything to add?

YAMA: Why would anyone steal?

DISCIPLE: Because they want something bad enough to take the risk of being caught, but fear they lack the means of purchasing it; or perhaps for the thrill of the adventure; or maybe even revenge and they feel justified? Perhaps survival?

YAMA: Delusion. One steals because they feel they lack something they need and that there is another to steal from. If they would come to the truth of their nature they would know that there is no need and that there is no other. Each person is but a member of the body of humanity, and the body of humanity is but a member of the body of the world where other species serve as other members. To steal from another is the same as the right hand taking from the left. However, due to the fear of being a little separated thing among so many other things one steals.

DISCIPLE: What about a mother taking fruit from a vendor to feed her hungry child, is that wrong?

YAMA: This is nothing about right and wrong. It is all a matter of attitude. No one owns anything after all. It is all God's. Does not the Creator have the rights to His creations?

180

DISCIPLE: Of course.

YAMA: There are some cultures that have no sense of personal property. They use whatever they might need for the time needed and then let it go for someone else to use. The idea of stealing to such people makes as much sense as feeling guilty when plucking an apple from a tree they happen upon. To such a people who have no sense of ownership there exists an inherent trust that the world will provide their simple needs.

DISCIPLE: So it's ok to take whatever one wants since nothing belongs to anyone anyway?

YAMA: Careful, the mind can argue from any direction and never touch the truth. Any teaching, any words, can be used to lead one deeper into illusion and misery.

Any fearful action will create fearful events. Cause and effect. If one acts in the state of peace then that is what one creates. To find God, who is always waiting and watching, one must develop trust. To take what has not been given generally implies lack of trust. Acting out of desperation to preserve the body is falling into the illusion of being a body, instead of being the Eternal Spirit that has no needs.

To eat your food, or to don your clothes, or to take your child to school without giving thanks to the Creator is stealing. Remember, there is nothing that you own. Give up the sense of ownership and surrender to the One who owns it all. In this way your mind will not steal away from the awareness that everything is God's and is God. Gratitude, instead of self-righteous pride of earning what one has acquired, will be fostered, and the Giver can then be remembered and is invited to be recognized with every action.

Then everything becomes a gift. When one sees everything as a gift then one acts accordingly.

DISCIPLE: How does one know when one has stolen the moment?

YAMA: Generally, when one becomes angry. Anger is a sign of not being united with the present circumstance and feeling thwarted from acquiring what one wants or expects. Anger cannot be present when gratitude prevails.

DISCIPLE: I guess when you really get down to the essential there is no difference between the last two commandments because they are both about being in love with the moment.

YAMA: Exactly.

I bowed to Yama and left him on the bench. I walked home, smiling. Whatever I gazed upon I saw with gratitude: whatever shape of a body, flowers, weeds, cigarette butts, clouds, it did not matter. And with each breath I gave thanks. When I reached home I touched my wife's hair and lifted my giggling child into my arms, and I thanked God for this moment of Eternity God had gifted me.

****

Upon a bench Yama and I sat quietly watching the coy swimming in the man-made pond. An ankh and a purple sphere overlooked the small waterfall trickling into the pool. We were sitting in a sanctuary dedicated to Isis, a temple to the Egyptian goddess stood behind us.

DISCIPLE: Yama, I find it ironic that we have come here to talk about the Commandments Moses was given after escaping Egypt.

YAMA: What applies to outside Egypt applies as well to inside. Sometimes it takes one to get out of civilization, to go into the wilderness, to come to right understanding.

DISCIPLE: True. However, what I was referring to specifically was the vehemence that Moses had had towards the goddess. After all, he did come down the mountain and soon ordered thousands of her worshippers slaughtered!

YAMA: I was indeed busy guiding away souls then. Yet be careful, nothing is ever as it seems to our senses. Great forces were present there, stirring up pools of energy that had become stagnant. Just as this pond here that we sit next to would quickly become covered with scum, choking the fish within eventually, if the waterfall ceased; so too does this happen to civilizations, religions, movements and individuals when new impulses are not allowed to stream in. When this stifling occurs it sometimes takes an unleashing of a dam that can appear very violent.

I looked at the waters trickling in the pond and visualized the stream stopping and the growing of the algae, and the sad plight of the fish. And while the algae is as much part of life as the fish, for this time and in this place, the living slime is a symbol of stagnation and decay, while the fish and their potency is the symbol of dynamic life; and that it would be right action to destroy the algae by whatever action to save the fish.

My being shuddered at the truth of this vision, for how many megalomaniacs with their armies would love to claim that they were doing God's Will as they slaughtered millions?

For a while we sat in the joyful tinkling of the waterfall, until two workers on the grounds began yelling at each other. My immediate thought was one of judgment—for should they not be following the Ideals of Ma'at, to keep their emotions balanced?

YAMA: So, what is the Ninth Commandment, for I believe that is where we're at?

DISCIPLE: Thou shall not falsely accuse thy neighbor.

YAMA: Are you not falsely accusing your neighbors right now?

I blushed.

DISCIPLE: I am accusing them of falling short of the precepts of their order. However, am I really falsely accusing them?

YAMA: Do you even know that they are of this order or are you assuming?

DISCIPLE: I must admit that I am assuming.

YAMA: With that accusation, that assumption, you have cut your mind off from God. You were sitting here in the Peace of Existence until your mind took charge, and wielding its sword of condemnation, you turned into these people's finger-wagging parent. And what happened to your peace?

DISCIPLE: I lost awareness of it.

YAMA: The same goes with your accusation of Moses committing genocide, that is based on only what the senses experience and then the mind extrapolating a moral judgment. This, like with most accusations, does not constitute right understanding.

DISCIPLE: Surely there exist proper accusations against those who are dong ill to others, such as with tyrannical leaders or criminals to name only a few? Without accusation many of our social reforms, such as women's rights or the civil rights movement, would never have come to pass.

YAMA: Indeed there is proper action to stand up against harmful actions and stagnant energy; but to judge your neighbor by those actions brings only suffering to you and your neighbor. You can never know all the reasons, the circumstances that have led any person to act as heinously as they do. Priests and psychoanalysts may give some reason or two as to the cause, but do they really have that all-knowing wisdom? Only those with utmost arrogance could claim so. To see the whys of the way of people one would have to see with purest of eyes, unblemished by any faults. That is why Jesus challenged anyone to cast the first stone at the prostitute if they were free of error. And what human has not erred?

Most people accuse because they are desperately trying to end their own suffering by finding causes of suffering out there, by finding fault with others instead of seeing their own. By making the world

184

free of those bad people out there, by the eradication of all the world's wrongs, then peace and happiness will come. Or so they think.

But it can never happen that way. The cause of suffering and happiness both lie within. Thus, accusing your neighbor, finding fault in him, keeps you from the Truth of seeing the Whole picture, and thus keeps your awareness from God.

If you really want to help your neighbor and make your world an amazing neighborhood, love him as he is, seeing beyond all his frail actions; so you and he can stand in the Truth of your Infinite Being where I cannot touch you as death.

And like the waterfall pouring oxygenated waters into the pond, so too did Yama's words fill my soul. I sent the two arguing people the thought that they were perfect as they were and that they were loved. And with that thought I felt again the Oneness I was part of and was; and did not notice when the argument had stopped.

******

Yama and I sat on the banks of the Russian River. A short way upriver teens and adults whooped and hollered as they frolicked on their various floating devices. The river brought them closer to disturb our solitude.

YAMA: Can they really disturb our solitude?

DISCIPLE: What do you mean? Here we are imbibing the silence of Nature and here they come popping their beers and completely disregarding the sanctity of the place.

YAMA: And what does that have to do with you?

DISCIPLE: It has everything to do with me!

I watched in horror as another flotilla of noise turned the bend.

185

DISCIPLE: I teach all week and have people at home who fight for my attention—All I want is a little piece and quiet.

YAMA: Like the old days when you were free and single, able to go anywhere as you pleased?

DISCIPLE: Well now that you mention it, I do at times miss those wandering days. It comes up at times, I must admit, when my brother, who has all this new freedom after becoming recently divorced, talks about his travels to exotic places.

YAMA: Are you to say then that you are envious of your brother?

I hesitated; then nodded my head.

YAMA: What was the reason you asked me here today?

DISCIPLE: For you to speak about the final Commandment.

YAMA: And what is the final Commandment that Moses brought down from the mountain?

DISCIPLE: "You shall not envy your neighbor, nor desire to have his house, his wife, his servants, his animals, nor anything that is his."

YAMA: Who is your neighbor but the one who lives next to you. Who is the one who lives next to you?—your brother (and I do not just mean your blood brother) who walks beside you.

Why do you think God asks us not to envy?

DISCIPLE: Because when I look at my envy for the wealth and freedom my brother has—or for that matter, envy of times when I sat by this river where no noisy revelers came to disturb me—I feel resentment.

YAMA: Good. Now you are speaking with some wisdom.

DISCIPLE: Maybe; but it is hard not to be envious at times. Just the other day I begged my friend to buy a painting because we are financially in need. Being a successful attorney he had no problem helping me out. Sometimes I am full of doubt about whether I chose the right road in careers when we have to move into a little place, while he lives in an expensive home and drives a car that doesn't break down like mine just did on the freeway the other day. Yes, I am envious!

I stood up, my face red with anger, and threw a stone into the river.

YAMA: Is your friend happy with his work? Are you aware of what he goes through every day to make his cash?

DISCIPLE: No to both questions. I know that at an early age he had a mild heart attack due to stress from his work.

YAMA: Do you envy that stress?

DISCIPLE: No, can't say that I do.

YAMA: So you just want the good stuff, but not the pain that walks as its shadow. People tend to look with envious eyes to their neighbors all around, whether the bigger house, the younger wife (or no wife, as the case may be), the nicer car, having/not having children, a different job, better education, nicer clothes, etc. Yet never do they even bother to consider what is going on with those they envy; such as, at what cost did it take to acquire that object of desire, or the cost of maintaining it? Or, getting right down to it, is the person even satisfied with what they have?

Your society, and the capitalism that guides most of you, is based on envy. It fosters envy with its ads that says that whatever you have is not good enough—there is something that is better. And this includes even body parts, for which you can get breast implants (though in your case I wouldn't recommend it) or get a penis enlargement (hmm … now maybe you could use …).

DISCIPLE: Ha, ha. Very funny!

YAMA: Would you trade your life for your brother or your friend's?

DISCIPLE: No, of course not.

YAMA: Each person is given whatever they need at any point in their lives. Some require more, some less. Their needs come as persons, things, actions, events. Some are pleasant while others the opposite.

People look at others riding high and sigh with longing, ignoring the pain that preceded the high and not willing to see the pain that will inevitably come as the Wheel of Life turns.

The instant you envy your brother you trade your life away for a wish. Your life and everyone's is as unique as a fingerprint. By being content in this moment, grateful that you even exist to be by this river, celebrating the fortunes of your friend and brother, you are free to achieve a happiness that no person, thing, or event could ever bestow upon you.

I threw another rock into the slow-moving waters. I watched as another group drifted our way. I sat down next to Yama and watched an orange and black beetle crawl up a blade of grass.

DISCIPLE: Does the beetle envy my life as a human? Do I envy the beetle and its freedom from responsibility? Would either of us trade places? No, I rather doubt it.

I let the beetle crawl onto my hand. Just then the group of rafters ran ashore just across from us, speaking loudly to each other in Portuguese.

I groaned.

YAMA: Would you trade places with someone else in a quieter place? Would you trade your life in for another condition, continuing the habit of trading one condition for another, and yet for another, until finally you obtain the perfect condition?

188

I shook my head.

YAMA: Do you love your life as it is?

I took a deep breath.

DISCIPLE: Yes. I love my life as it is.

YAMA: Good. Now sit back and enjoy your life exactly how it's meant to be.

I watched in horror as the Brazilians pulled out a massive radio. They hit the switch and meringue music blasted forth.

I could have cried. I could have cussed. Instead, a blissful feeling came over me and I just laughed. It was perfect! I looked over to Yama who was tapping his foot.

DISCIPLE: Hell, shall we dance?

Addendum II
Suicide, marijuana, Grace

I sat upon a grassy knoll overlooking a crowd of friends and other members of a community where I had been teaching for three years. There was a stage set up with a collage of pictures of one of the parents of a student of mine. Her family sat on the stage, their eyes red from crying. Her two adolescent children were sitting with friends on the grass.

YAMA: So, why the clenched jaws? It's like you are sitting in a jury box and listening to the grim details of a crime.

DISCIPLE: I guess it is like a crime—murder, in fact. How could she take such a cowardly way out of this life and leave her two children motherless? What the hell kind of template is that going to be for them to follow through the challenges of life. For months she planned her death and even wrote it down in her datebook.

So, yes, this was a pre-meditated murder of her God-given body.

YAMA: Aren't we judge and jury. So do you know all the facts of this case?

DISCIPLE: I know she was battling manic-depression for many years—since high school, according to her family. She went to therapy but would smoke pot to self-medicate, despite the warnings of her psychiatrist. I guess what burns me is when her friends come up and speak lightly of the fact she smoked marijuana to help with her condition.

YAMA: Why do you feel so?

DISCIPLE: Because pot destroys the will. I should know. I saw it in my brother as he became consumed by drugs, with pot as the forerunner, and I saw it in myself. Her will to push through the rough times could only be impotent with such chronic smoking. And another thing that pisses me off, besides the fact of leaving

190

behind those two great kids, is that she was very spiritual—a yoga practitioner!—and she knows you can't escape in this way.

Right? There's no escape, yes?

YAMA: Do you want to hear what I have to say or are you already locked in your judgment? If you are locked in I will not waste my time and will simply leave and do work elsewhere.

DISCIPLE: I want to listen.

YAMA: Before I begin you need to find your center, so you can truly hear.

Close your eyes and take a deep breath, imagining white light coming down like a shaft through the top of your head, and a shaft of white light rising up through the spine, meeting at your heart. Hold the breath, that light, at the heart. Then exhale that light to all present, including B. Repeat the inhalation and exhalation of the of light of God, of which no judgment can ever be found.

I began to breathe. At first it was hard as my mind kept screaming at her, but then, slowly, the ranting subsided and I could see her face lit with that light. And tears began to fall. And in that light I could see my dead brother's face as well.

YAMA: When we forgive a person we do so much more, so many more are included in that extinguishing of the fire of judgment.

Everyone has their path, and that may even include suicide, drug-addiction (which is but another form of suicide), all in the pursuit of finding happiness. In truth, such attempts are no different than a person looking for happiness by acquiring goods or living in a giant house or by being in positions of power, by having lots of sexual partners, and so on. They will find that all these activities will fail. Nothing can bring one happiness, no condition can do so. All such activity is but a vain search for completion. And only when one is complete is one alive.

When one is incomplete one is nothing more than a ghost, haunted by the specter of separation.

DISCIPLE: But isn't suicide the worst one could do? There are so many religious doctrines that warn against the dire consequences of taking one's life.

YAMA: The reason suicide is perhaps more painful is due to the guilt surrounding that act and all the fear due to such doctrines. When you die, or appear to do so, it is really no different than going to sleep, When you go to sleep happy, you will have happy dreams, and you will wake up happy and have a happy tomorrow. It is a cycle—a happy cycle. If you go to bed, on the other hand, depressed, full of fear and anxiety, your dreams will amount to the same and you will wake up to a tomorrow no better. The same with dying. But instead of days we have subtle realms and lifetimes.

DISCIPLE: How to get out of such a dark loop?

YAMA: Love. This is where the loved ones, those who can stand as witnesses to the divine truth of who that person really is, can send their blessings. Each blessing, each loving thought sent to the one who is suffering is a balm for his or her tormented mind. Each blessing is a whispering that says, *You are loved. You are love.*

DISCIPLE: I guess what I was doing, sitting here and yelling at her with my mind, wasn't exactly helpful, but was the opposite.

YAMA: Not only do such condemnations reinforce her own guilt-ridden image of herself, but it will put you on that dark cycle as well, and you both will sit in hell.

Do you not feel better now than when you were first sitting here?

DISCIPLE: Night and day. I literally felt on fire feeling so pissed off. Now I am lighter as I have let your words sink into my soul.

We sat for a while listening to friends talk about B's love for skiing and her body work that I had the pleasure of experiencing, and the

192

love she had for her children. I sighed at that last statement and sent her a thought that she was loved and is love.

DISCIPLE: What about marijuana? Am I right in my feelings about it?

YAMA: Cannabis, like all of the flora of the Earth, is a gift. Every weed has medicinal properties. And many weeds, when not used properly, can be harmful. Cannabis is such. There are times when the will needs to be stilled so other energies can enter the mind or the body to bring wisdom or healing. That is why cannabis has been used by shamans and holy men to help gain visions.

The danger comes in the addiction to the visions. Visions are there to inspire action in this material world. They are not there for entertainment. You will see many who suckle upon that drug and will live in a television of delusion, as they have no more will to move in the world. Lotus eaters they become. They will believe all is well, (which is the truth), but not in a real way which entails going into the shadows of oneself and eventually come to see the light.

DISCIPLE: Well, I was well on my way to becoming such a lotus eater.

YAMA: And how did you overcome that propensity?

DISCIPLE: One day it just ended, along with my drinking. That desire to drink and to partake in any kind on mind-altering substance just disappeared.

YAMA: That is called Grace. By your yearning for God and knowing such habits were impediments, and calling upon the Masters you became connected to, you invoked help outside of the you you believed yourself to be. And in an instant your life was changed. Such is the timeless power of Grace.

And such is the reminder of the invisible help that is always there for the asking.

DISCIPLE: And I am so grateful for that Grace. And having known that Grace I have the utmost faith that it is there waiting whenever I need it again.

YAMA: It is there all the time, assisting, guiding, in unseen ways. Now send that Grace to her mind, and know that in just such an instant, she needs stay no longer in her hell. Where you are standing now you are her witness of who she really is, not what she appears to be. See past the veil with the One Eye of Knowing and recognize that she is already free.

I closed my eyes to the sound of music being played down below, tunes that B had loved, and sent her God's loving Grace. And I could see in my mind's eye, her getting up from her dark cell and move to the iron barred door; and then open it and step out to find herself on top of a mountain. She stood on skis and held her poles, with her two children to the sides of her, also similarly outfitted. Then down the pure white snow of the mountain the three of them screamed down in outright joy.

To B, and to Robin, and to all those who forgot but for an instant of time in Eternity.

ABOUT THE AUTHOR

Janaka Stagnaro resides in Sacramento, California, where he teaches in a Wadorf-inspired public school and lives with his wife and their third grader. He loves doing art, storytelling, exploring Nature and playing games.

Other Book Titles by Janaka Stagnaro

ℰ *Beyond the Beyond: Poems to my Beloved Self*
ℰ *Footprints Along the Shore of an Incoming Tide: Impressions of a Fellow Traveler*
ℰ *Silent Ripples: Parables for the Soul*

Web Works by Janaka Stagnaro

ℰ *Mindfulness-Meditation-Techniques.com*
ℰ *TriLiving: Celebrating Truth, Beauty and Goodness*
ℰ JanakasArt on Artfire.com

Made in the USA
Monee, IL
11 November 2021